Thinking of ...

Offering a Cloud Solution?

Ask the Smart Questions

By Ian Gotts and Stephen Parker

Proudly sponsored by:

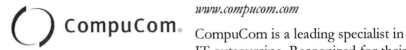

www.compucom.com

CompuCom is a leading specialist in IT outsourcing. Recognized for their unique Integrated Infrastructure Management™ (IIM) solution, CompuCom helps clients reduce costs, increase productivity through innovation, and drive greater business value from their IT infrastructure.

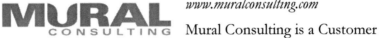

www.muralconsulting.com

Mural Consulting is a Customer Experience Agency that helps businesses to successfully engage their customers online and support them throughout the 10-phase, Web-Centric Customer Life-Cycle, from attracting prospects to creating advocates.

NIMBUS

from strategy to reality

www.nimbuspartners.com

Nimbus is a business process content management software vendor which helps clients drive the adoption of business change, by delivering process-related content to the entire workforce via the web, Microsoft Sharepoint, the iPhone or WinMobile device.

www.nitrosell.com

NitroSell enables small-to-midsize brick-and-mortar retailers to increase sales and profits by implementing and running integrated online stores, no matter where in the world they are.

www.nspi.com

NSPI has years of experience managing complex, business critical infrastructures for customers of all sizes in North America. It is recognized for industry certified expertise and flexible Managed Hosted Service offerings.

Smart Questions™ Philosophy

Smart Questions is built on 4 key pillars, which set it apart from other publishers:

1. *Smart people want Smart Questions not Dumb Answers*

2. *Domain experts are often excluded from authorship, so we are making writing a book simple and painless*

3. *The community has a great deal to contribute to enhance the content*

4. *We donate a percentage of revenue to a charity voted for by the authors and community. It is great marketing, but it is also the right thing to do*

www.Smart-Questions.com

Reviews

The whole "Thinking of" series focusing on the Smart Questions is a brilliant concept. These books encourage an informed debate rather than prescribing a specific path which may not be the right one for your business. This book is an invaluable resource for ISVs. The authors have done a great job in articulating the opportunities and the challenges ISVs face in this transition to a Software plus Services world. Although targeted at ISVs, in my view, it is equally valuable for customers so they can assess the capability of their software suppliers in providing resilient and capable Cloud services.

Gurprit Singh, Director Emerging Technologies, Microsoft

www.microsoft.com

Salesforce.com, with its Force.com platform, has always believed in the power of Cloud Computing to deliver enterprise scale apps to businesses of every size. We see it every day with our 60,000 customers. What Ian and Stephen have put together is the most comprehensive list of all the questions that an ISV should answer before 'launching into the Clouds'.

Tim Knight, Senior Director, Force.com

www.Salesforce.com

Ian and Stephen have written an insightful book that takes a refreshing research-driven approach to helping businesses understand, navigate and take advantage of this dynamic Cloud Compute market. Ask the Smart Questions provides practical advice on how to stay nimble and flexible in an ever-morphing cloud landscape and offers a paint-by-numbers Q&A session for decision makers looking to transform themselves and successfully claim a stake in the 'Cloud pie'.

Steve O'Deegan, Managing Partner, Laurel Group

www.laurel-group.com

Ian and Stephen have created a great handbook for all software developers looking to build solutions in the Cloud. If you are a software developer planning a Cloud Computing solution, then this book should be part of your planning process. If you are a software developer who hasn't yet thought about how you will address the opportunity and threat that Cloud Computing creates for you, then Thinking of offering a Cloud solution is a great place to start and could help you to not be left behind by your peers. Whichever you are, answer the questions in Chapters 8 and 9 carefully as they are based on real world experience that has seen others succeed and fail. If you ignore any of these key questions, you will only have to answer them later and that could be too late.

Jeremy Roche, Chief Executive, CODA
www.coda2go.com

This book offers ISVs a great entry into the new world of S+S. Ever wondered how, why or what? If so then the questions in this book and the thought it provokes are for you as it will stimulate your decisions as you consider moving all or part of your business to Software+Services.

Richard Phillips, ISV Partner Manager, Microsoft

www.microsoft.com

An ISV usually realizes that moving to the Cloud isn't optional, before they come to Navatar Group for help. The ISV doesn't realize, however, that simply Cloud-enabling their On-Premise software won't translate into a profitable business model. We recommend this book as a 'must-read' for every ISV so you can make an informed choice between selling a 'product' and providing a 'service', based on your customer needs and your ability to change. Answering the Smart Questions will provide a basis for a realistic cost benefit analysis as well as help you understand what will resonate with your customers and where you will need advice or partnerships.

Alok Misra, Principal, Navatar Group

www.navatargroup.com

Authors

Ian Gotts

Founder and CEO of Nimbus, which has been offering their process management solution as a Cloud Computing offering to major corporations for the last 4 years. This was a transition made from the traditional model. Now over 70% of new customers have used the Nimbus service including Toyota, SAP, Cognos, Nestle, HM Revenue & Customs and HSBC Bank.

He is author of 3 books, *Common Approach, Uncommon Results* and *Why Killer Products Don't Sell* and *Thinking of… Buying Cloud Computing? Ask the Smart Questions* which makes him a sought after conference speaker.

Stephen Parker

A business executive, with over 20 years experience of taking critical technology investment decisions and delivering solutions on the leading edge of IT in large enterprises, '.com' start-ups, and business turnarounds. His recent journey of turning around a struggling ERP vendor into a leading Cloud Computing business in the eProcurement space and taking this to a trade sale has added scars and knowledge in equal measures.

His down to earth approach, backed up by real-life experience and an ability to bridge the gap between board room strategy and the depths of technology, provides him with a rare insight into the world of Cloud Computing. He is the author of *Thinking of… Buying Cloud Computing? Ask the Smart Questions* and consults to companies considering Cloud Computing and to analyst firms focused in this space.

Table of Contents

Acknowledgements

The Cloud which is making these changes possible has been funded by a range or organizations. Too many to list. But they know who they are. And they and their investors should be proud of what they have achieved, even if it hasn't shown up on the balance sheet.

This book is being made available by the generous sponsorship of a few companies who are committed to making a Cloud approach possible for their customers. Our thanks should go to them.

But the best way to thank them is to read the book and take action.

Foreword

Cloud Computing – threat of opportunity? We see existing software developers are missing the impact that Cloud Computing could have on their business. This is a grave error.

Any seismic shift in technology resets the clock. This gives a new start-up the ability to launch a new idea which delivers exceptional business value. And the speed that they can be brought to market is like nothing we have seen before. This poses a huge threat to the established players, mired in the only paradigm of on-premise software. They have the protection of scale, track record and customer trust. But that won't protect them in every account. Cloud Computing enables a 'young turk' to get a pilot implementation of their software into a strategic account and grow it from there.

We've already see the major industry players responding. Microsoft, who has enviable margins for its desktop and server products, is investing massively to bring those to market as a Cloud Computing service. It is cannibalizing itself before someone else does. The same is true for the other industry giants.

But what of the small and mid-market software ISVs? "How will they respond?" is not the question to be answered. "How MUST they respond?" is the real question to be asked. Given the implications of moving all or part of their solution to a Cloud Computing model it will take time. Time to create the strategy. Time to plan the migration. Time to redevelop the solution. That could be 6 to 18 months before the solution is available as a credible Cloud Computing service. So they'd better get started.

But it is not only relevant to the established players. Those young start-ups have their own challenges. The Cloud Computing business models are still evolving. There are few good role models. There are critical strategic business decisions to be made to ensure that business can scale profitably, and build real business value. Many of the questions in the book challenge some of the myths of Cloud Computing.

That is why this book is so valuable. It can help you create your strategy. Reading it may make you feel depressed or euphoric about the potential of Cloud Computing, but scared of getting started. That is the wrong reaction. The beauty of this book is that it lists all the concerns that you could possibly have – although not all of them will be relevant to your situation.

Ian and Stephen have pulled together a great book on the subject of offering a Cloud Computing solution and brought it to life with some real life case studies. My plea to you is to read the book, think carefully about the Smart Questions and use them to make equally smart decisions in your organization. And make sure that you are one of the leaders in the next wave of computing.

Darren Bibby (Program Director, IDC Software Channels Research)

Who should read this book?

People like you and me

This book is aimed squarely at the established Independent Software Vendor (ISV) who is considering the Cloud as a route to market for their software offerings. However, this book is not deeply technical, nor was it ever intended to be.

And whilst a new software start-up does not have the legacy issues of the established ISV, many of the questions in the book will enable them to create a winning strategy from day one. It should enable them to eliminate some of the trips down blind alleys that are normally associated with any new venture.

This book is intended to be a catalyst for action aimed at a range of people inside and outside your organization. Here are just a few, and why it is relevant to them:

Chief Executive Officer

As CEO you are responsible for the overall performance of the business. That means setting strategy. You are probably watching with interest the debate around Cloud Computing as a term. You can probably bet that your customers are looking at it as an option to increase availability, increase flexibility or reduce cost.

Understanding the Smart Questions will allow you to formulate your strategy to migrate your solutions into the Cloud.

Chief Executive Officer of a start-up

You are probably looking at Cloud Computing as a way of getting to market quickly and effectively. But is it the right long term strategy? What are the risks inherent in this strategy? Will it support or hamper your speed to market and your long term growth?

This book will help you ask the Smart Questions, because if you don't it may cost you the company.

Head of Sales

You've seen more nimble Cloud Computing service providers running rings around your sales team who only have an on-premise offering. But you have a number of existing customers. Will you cannibalize on-premise sales at the expense of a smaller but longer term annuity revenue? How do you organize, manage and motivate your sales teams? How to you manage the inevitable channel conflict? What are the new metrics to manage the sales business?

This book will help you plan a marketing and sales strategy to take advantage of Cloud Computing.

Head of Development

You deliver stable software in regular controlled releases. Not always exciting. But you are not paid to be exciting. You are paid to be calm and collected. Is Cloud Computing going to change that, and how? What is the best architecture to take advantage of Cloud Computing, and is this a complete re-write or a series of evolutionary steps?

This book will help you understand what is required, and how you can benefit from the new world of Cloud Computing.

Chief Operations Officer

Cloud Computing will change the way you run the operation. Suddenly you have more moving parts. Before it was well defined. Build a product. Sell it. Ship it. Support it. Now you are responsible for keeping a part of your customer's IT operation running 24 x 7. What are the risks? What are the costs involved? Can you even make money? Is Cloud Computing just going to make the place even more difficult to run or will it create opportunities?

Asking the Smart Questions, so that you get the right answers will help you assess the impact of Cloud Computing.

Chief Finance Officer

They say Cloud Computing is easier to sell so will reduce the cost of sales and up the win ratio. But you're used to healthy margins, which look to be slashed in exchange for the promise of long term annuity revenues. Is it a reasonable or even sensible trade-off? How is the company going to fund the transition and the inevitable chaos until the business settles down? Does the business plan need to be torn up, and if it does what do you base the new plan on?

This book will give you a sound understanding of the areas to question.

Investor

So you've invested in an interesting company which is now deciding to embark on a Cloud Computing strategy. Is it a clever move or the beginning of the end? How do you evaluate the new business plans and budgets? How can you offer the best advice and support?

This book offers the Smart Questions you need to ask to help you assess the impact of Cloud Computing.

How to use this book

This book is intended to be the catalyst for action. We hope that the ideas and examples inspire you to act. So, do whatever you need to do to make this book useful. Use Post-it notes, photocopy pages, scan pages, and write on it. Go to our website and email colleagues the e-book summary. Rip it apart, or read it quickly in one sitting. Whatever works for you. We hope this becomes your most dog-eared book.

Clever clogs – skip to the questions

Some of you understand the background to Cloud Computing and have a pretty good grasp of the implications, benefits and risks. Therefore you have permission to skip to Chapter 7 where the structure of the questions is explained.

But before you go, please read 'Getting Involved' on the next page. You can always come back to Chapters 1-6 later.

Getting Involved

The Smart Questions community

There may be questions that we should have asked but didn't. Or specific questions which may be relevant to your situation, but not everyone in general. Go to the website for the book and post the questions. You never know, they may make it into the next edition of the book. That is a key part of the Smart Questions Philosophy.

Send us your feedback

We love feedback. We prefer great reviews, but we'll accept anything that helps take the ideas further. We welcome your comments on this book.

We'd prefer email, as it's easy to answer and saves trees. If the ideas worked for you, we'd love to hear your success stories. Maybe we could turn them into 'Talking Heads'-style video or audio interviews on our website, so others can learn from you. That's one of the reasons why we wrote this book. So talk to us.

feedback@Smart-Questions.com

Got a book you need to write?

Maybe you are a domain expert with knowledge locked up inside you. You'd love to share it and there are people out there desperate for your insights. But you don't think you are an author and don't know where to start. Making it easy for you to write a book is part of the Smart Questions Philosophy.

Let us know about your book idea, and let's see if we can help you get your name in print.

potentialauthor@Smart-Questions.com

Chapter

Clouds forming

We all live under the same sky, but we don't all have the same horizon.

Konrad Adenauer (German Statesman, 1876-1967)

Storm clouds

L OOKING at the resignation letter on my desk, I'm don't understand how we got it so wrong. He is our top salesman and was the most vocal about offering a Cloud solution alongside our existing product. And now he's joining our biggest competitor, who haven't considered the Cloud. Why?

Execution was clearly the issue. The strategy was correct but our implementation was a disaster as new issues kept surprising us. We underestimated how this new offering confused customers. We thought they understood Cloud Computing. It simply stalled sales. They assumed they need less consulting support and projects started to fail, so then the help desk was swamped and customer satisfaction scores went through the floor.

But the worst was the sales cannibalization and changing salesmen's compensation to be tied into our annuity model. And that, it seems, was the last straw for our salesmen. If they can't make money, they will go somewhere where they can.

12 months ago, before we launched our Cloud Computing strategy we were on the top of our game. Now we are fighting for survival.

There are so many questions, with hindsight, we wish we'd asked.

Cloud Computing: a definition

Cloud Computing is the in-vogue name for the model of providing software from a remote location, over a network, where the organization using the software does not have to be involved with the day to day running of it.

It clearly has great benefits, but also comes with risks[1]. But not all the risks are that obvious hence the need for this book. But first we need to agree some definitions.

Originally the generally accepted term was Software as a Service. The use of the word service was based on the association with other 'services' that we just use without being concerned about the complexities behind the scenes For example, the telephone, the supply of electricity, the use of our Visa card.

As more people have started writing about and promoting the approach there has been an SAE[2] making it difficult to differentiate between SaaS, PaaS, S+S, DaaS, ASP, On-Demand or Utility. So in this book we are going to use 'Cloud Computing' which seems to be the umbrella term that is gaining traction and is being used almost universally. The new term is based on the services being provided by servers which are in the Cloud.

The opposite of this approach is referred to as on-premise, where, as the name suggests the hardware and software are installed and run within an organization. Today this is still by some way the dominant approach.

There is a long history of the IT industry providing models where software can be delivered as a service from a central location, and one could even argue that this goes right back to the mainframe days (plus ca change, plus c'est la meme chose). Terms such as eBusiness, on demand, utility computing, ASP and so forth have been marketed since the mid 90's. All have had the same basic message that you should not have to worry about looking after the infrastructure for delivering your software, you should just get on and use it.

---

[1] No such thing as a free lunch etc

[2] SAE - Significant Acronym Explosion!

Terminology

There are many terms being bandied around to describe this approach. Below are just some of them:

- SaaS : Software as a Service

- PaaS : Platform as a Service

- DaaS : Data as a Service

- ASP : Application Service Provider

- Hosted

- Software + Services : On-premise software + hosted services

- On-Demand

- Web 2.0

- Utility Computing

We will be using 'Cloud Computing' as a generic umbrella term for all of these.

Naturally as time has passed, refinements are being offered to this simple, everything 'On-Premise' or everything 'in the Cloud' story. Microsoft in particular has advocated the concept of a hybrid model that they refer to as Software plus Services. The idea is that the best solutions will combine the benefits of on-premise software with the advantages of services delivered via the web.

And whilst this may have started as marketing or positioning, in reality it is really the logical architectural approach, given that the mobile workforce cannot guarantee being connected 100% of the time.

Cloud Computing is evolving and there is a growing list of synonyms to cover various elements of the paradigm. One is the notion of 'Multi Tenant' architecture for the software. This is the concept of one installation of the software having many customers using it, each with their data and configuration segregated by the software. Like a building with multiple self-contained apartments with multiple tenants. However this is not the only approach. Virtualization allows many installations of a standard 'application environment' on the same physical server, allowed a 'virtual dedicated' environment per customer.

The future is here

Some say that the future is already here, but it is unevenly distributed.

By that we mean that if you look around you can find examples of any new innovation being used in anger, delivering business benefits, it's just that not everyone is using it. Recently Information Age highlighted 10 Cloud Computing business success stories. What is interesting is they are all using the Cloud equivalent of packaged applications. You could argue that Japan Post is the exception as they are using a Cloud service – Force.com – to extend the core CRM and build applications.

Information Age business success stories

Information Age in March 2009 listed its view of the some of the business success stories, and here they are:

Japan Post: Using Force.com they developed a data consolidation system in 3 months and rolled it out to 65,000 users in 24,000 branches.

Santander Consumer Finance: Uses Service-Now.com IT Service Management at a fraction of the cost of their previous on-premise application.

Roche: Adopted a Cloud Computing talent management service from Taleo dramatically improving its reputation with potential graduate candidates.

GE: Managing 50,000 suppliers using multiple apps was a challenge, so when it wanted to consolidate it chose Aravo as it supported the scale GE needed.

ACAL Technology: Whilst reorganizing its international sales operation decided to provide better tools for office and field team and chose NetSuite.

Osborne Clarke: The law firm's email service was under attack so they implemented Mimecast which was significantly cheaper than an in-house alternative.

Abbot Medical Optics: To improve the visibility of its expense management they turned to Concur as they could cope with the multi-country tax complexity.

Chiquita: Its legacy HR could not cope with the scale of operation; 24,000 employees in 70 countries. Workday beat off the on-premise offerings.

Thomas Cook: RightNow's CRM system was so friendly it was the choice for the single customer service bank for their call centre and home-based agents.

THK-BP: Reducing contract approval from 12 hours to 6 and reducing admin overhead was a key benefit of implementing OILspace Energy Trade Risk app.

The new infrastructure players

There are companies making big bets around Cloud Computing and developing the infrastructure that ISVs can use make the migration more quickly. Accenture Technology Labs compared the top 6 players in a recent report. "What the Enterprise Needs to Know About Cloud Computing". An excerpt of the results is in the Appendix.

But their results carry a Health Warning, which they make clear in their opening paragraphs. Cloud Computing is evolving at a pace so anything which discusses the specifics of any platform will rapidly become out of date[3]. Nevertheless here are some perspectives on a few of the players.

Salesforce.com & Force.com

Often held up as the poster child for Cloud Computing, it was not the first, nor is it the largest. It is a significant company with great reach and a compelling vision which has only starting to play out with its development platform. What made it the poster child was its powerful PR and the original tagline of 'No software'. That line is not really true now, as they offer the ability to work offline with locally installed software either on the PC or the mobile device.

What is making Salesforce.com's long term potential as one of the major software players so exciting is Force.com. Force.com has 'drag and drop' tools that allow a business-user to build a new business system (such as HR or Operations). It has a development environment where systems engineers can code complex logic, validation, workflow and screen designs to make that simple business system come to life. And it provides all this through a hosted platform.

---

[3] Fortunately the questions in this book are not tied to technology solutions so they have a longer lifespan.

Microsoft Azure

Microsoft is often accused of coming late to any party. What they cannot be faulted for is the immense investment that they are prepared to make once they decide to join the party, and how patient they are to get a result. Microsoft Azure is their 'Cloud Computing platform in the sky' enabling anyone with a correctly designed Microsoft application to run it from the 'Cloud' for their customers.

But Azure could be just a part of an ISV's product strategy. Some locally installed software for power users and the engaging Web2.0 access which needs to be global and scalable on Azure. And perhaps some of the heavy-lift analysis, processing and reporting load which is very peaky could be Azure which can spool up servers to match demand.

With this you can see how Azure plays an integral part of Microsoft's Software plus Services strategy and how it supports the 'Power of Choice' message for customers.

Amazon

Amazon was one of the few companies launched in the dotcom era that has made it. They are an example of selling the 'Long Tail' which the internet has made possible and financially viable. But they are 100% on-line. No internet connection means no access.

As an e-commerce site they need to have the computing capacity to cope with peaks in demand, such as the last minute Christmas purchases. As this capacity is largely unused during other times, they have launched a service called EC2, 'Elastic Cloud Compute'. Put simply, they are making their servers available, at a cost, for anyone who has an application that they want run from the Cloud.

Chapter

2

Opportunity?

Don't wait. The time will never be just right.

Napoleon Hill (author, 1883 – 1970)

SO why should I be interested? The Cloud Computing evangelists would have us all believe that this is the only future and someday soon all software will be delivered as a service. And looking at the huge investments that some of the largest 'gorillas' in the IT industry are making, maybe there is something to this.

However putting on one side the hyperbole that always goes hand in hand with new ideas in IT, there are in fact many sound reasons to consider this approach.

Maybe we are years away, but what is 60 years in 'Cloud-time'?

It took electricity 60 years to move to the Cloud model; why should software be any different?

A hundred years ago, companies stopped generating their own power with steam engines and dynamos and plugged into the newly built electric grid. The cheap power pumped out by electric utilities didn't just change how businesses operate. It set off a chain reaction of economic and social transformations that brought the modern world into existence. Today, a similar revolution is under way. Hooked up to the Internet's global computing grid, massive information-processing plants have begun pumping data and software code into our homes and businesses. This time, it's computing that's turning into a utility.

Summary of the book *The Big Switch* by Nicholas Carr.

Enterprise capability at commodity costs

By providing the service to multiple customers, utilizing a common centralized infrastructure, you can achieve economies of scale and therefore provide the service at a reduced cost compared to an on-premise solution. Also by 'outsourcing' the service provision there will be the potential for internal cost savings.

However, this requires a huge investment in capabilities that typically go beyond what an ISV could afford to or would want to deploy. For example, redundant servers, on-site spares, multiple data centers supporting disaster recovery, 24 hr security guards, enterprise versions of software (rather than standard), a team of technical specialists, sophisticated backup etc. But there are hosting companies providing these capabilities at commodity costs, allowing you in turn to offer creative commercial arrangements to your customers.

Freed from the financial constraints of purchasing servers, connectivity, back-up and all the supporting costs we should expect to see very innovative ISVs launching using Cloud Computing as the platform. But best of all you don't need to be large and well-funded. This new model means that a very capable looking system could be just two of you in the dorm room at college. But have you considered how you are going to provide support in between lectures and out partying?

Speed of availability vs. implementation

Because the service is already installed and waiting for use, much of the traditional time taken for customers to plan, install, configure and deploy is removed. This can allow them to have rapid access to sophisticated services and start achieving the business benefits as soon as possible. But don't confuse availability with their ability to use the service. There will be changes in the way they work. There will be manual activities. There may be specific ways that they want the service used. Simply making the service available, unless it is very simple and of a very narrow scope, will result in chaos.

Anywhere Access

Due to the centralized nature of the service, it no longer matters where you are as long as you can access the internet (at least occasionally). Sophisticated mobile devices (Blackberry, iPhone, Windows Mobile etc.) have further pushed this idea by providing access to email and company data wherever you are in the world.

The hybrid models such as Software plus Services are also providing answers to the "What happens when not connected to the internet" question by providing synchronized copies of data, which is managed centrally by the 'service', to the local device's 'software'. But this has implications on the architectural complexity of the solutions you need to develop.

Always up to date

The centralized management of the services makes it easier for you to deploy updates and once deployed all users will have access to the new capabilities. This also provides the opportunity to have more frequent release cycles, which leads to a more rapid introduction of improvements, bug fixes and enhancement requests. This means that you can move to truly agile development.

Salesforce.com: A new day and what new functionality has appeared?

When Salesforce.com first launched in the UK, for early customers the service was a fairly basic CRM solution; accounts, contacts, opportunities and reporting. But that was perfect. Most customers were migrating from using Outlook and were small.

But Salesforce.com had grander ambitions and had a development team back in San Francisco working hard to extend the functionality. Therefore each new release meant that users would come in to discover new tabs had appeared, such as campaigns, or a few new fields in the contacts tabs or new screen designs. No warning, no ability to preview and test. Bang, it was there.

Now Salesforce.com is far more sophisticated and mature. You have the ability to control which tabs and fields an end user sees and the screen layouts. There is a sandbox for testing prior to making new functionality available. That means that customers now control the implementation of new functionality, not Salesforce.com. But they get the benefit of providing one code base to all users around the world.

This requires a far more sophisticated system that the one first launched 5 years ago. Fortunately, Salesforce.com now is a very mature and capable service.

This is in sharp contrast to the traditional on-premise model with one or two updates a year. Many customers don't deploy these updates due to the business disruption and overhead involved and hence they don't get the benefits of the new release.

Maturity

Although there is always room for improvement, the reliability, security and capability of the 'Cloud services' is in general 'good enough'. As the music industry has found to its surprise, people have been happy to accept the quality compromises of the portable MP3 format, because of the huge gains in convenience and reduced cost[4].

For Cloud Computing, the presence of industry heavy weights such as Google, Oracle, Microsoft et al, further reinforces the validity of the market. Maturity will come, but until it does there are opportunities for new start-ups to steal a march on existing players.

Music trends show the impact of the web on record company's business models

The music industry has grown accustomed to dismal sales numbers, and in 2008 even the good news comes with disappointment. "Tha Carter III" is the first release in SoundScan's 17-year history to top the year-end list with sales of fewer than 3 million.

Sales of digital music continued to rise steeply. Just over a billion songs were downloaded, a 27 percent increase from 2007, and some record companies say they are finally beginning to wring significant profits from music on web sites like YouTube and MySpace. But analysts say that despite the growth and promise of digital music — in 2003 just 19 million songs were purchased as downloads — the money made online is still far from enough to make up for losses in physical sales.

"As the digital side grows, you get a different business model, with more revenue streams," said Michael McGuire, an analyst with Gartner, a market research firm. "But do we get back to where the revenue that the labels see is going to be fully replacing the CD in the next four to five years? No." Gartner recently issued a report urging record companies to put their primary focus on downloads.

---

[4] I'm not suggesting free (ripped) but buying by the track, rather than a CD

Chapter 3

Threat?

Advertising - a judicious mixture of flattery and threats.

Northrop Frye (literary theorist, 1912– 1991)

THE language is emotional, revolutionary and is inciting a disruptive change across the industry. It suggests that the only winners will be the new players who embrace the Cloud full-on. But is this the only way? Surely not.

Looking at the huge investments that the largest players in the IT industry are making, Cloud Computing is clearly something should be taken as a serious threat.

Low barriers, quick to market

For a start-up there could never have been a better time. With the Web 2.0 development tools, building an application is becoming easier and quicker. Leveraging the infrastructure provided the big players they can provide a credible service which is global and scalable from day one. Suddenly the need to raise $10m of venture capital to get going has gone[5].

---

[5] Which is lucky because so have many of the sources of funding.

Startups have no track record or credibility. But the flip side is that they also have no legacy or concerns of cannibalization of sales from existing customers. They can launch with new pricing and revenue models which are very compelling to customers – in some cases that means free.

This is highly threatening to established ISVs. And whilst the startup will not take the entire market it can certainly disrupt. At best, they can target the ISV's strategic customers, snipe, dodge, weave, get lucky, and maybe get a small implementation. From there they can grow – like a parasite. The word is well chosen because in the natural world, the nature of a parasite is to not make itself known. A smart parasite lives without being detected because if it is detected, of course, something is going to be done to eradicate it. This will hit sales and margins. For existing ISVs, farming existing customers should be the most profitable sales. The new start-up's pricing and offering will start the customer asking some awkward questions and stall your sales.

Change is never easy

Talk me though it: You want to spend time, money and disrupt the organization to move to a product offering which is higher risk, is more complex as it includes service delivery, is less profitable and hits cash flow. And you'd rather spend time and money on this, rather than adding more revenue generating capabilities to the core products or driving more business. Sorry. Not convinced.

However, doing nothing is the biggest risk. Innovation is critical to sustainable success. Apple innovates aggressively so that it obsoletes its own products rather than wait for a new entrant to steal a march.

But it is very difficult to launch a new product when the existing business is going so well. This is what Charles Handy calls The Sigmoid Curve or Second Curve thinking in his excellent book *The Empty Raincoat*[6]. Handy suggests that any product (like life, an empire, or a business) starts slowly and builds up, peaks and declines.

---

[6] A summary is in the Appendix

But way before it peaks, at Point A in the diagram below, you need to be developing the next product because it will take time to get up to speed. But how do you know where Point A is? It should be before the original product peaks, but how can we know when that is? The perfect time is probably when all the messages are that the original product is going well and still accelerating. Only once the product starts to decline do we know that we should have started the new product some months earlier. But by then it's too late. See the problem? And Cloud Computing is at Point A for many ISVs.

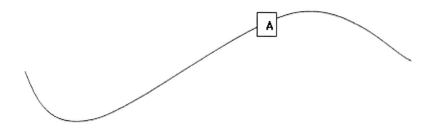

It's a paradox in some ways, when we say the time to change is when things are going well. But as Bill Shankly, the late great and very successful Liverpool football club manager once famously said: "Always change a winning team".

Beginning of the end or end of the beginning?

Does this mean that thousands of existing ISVs will go out of business? Not necessarily. But it does mean that there will be a great deal of soul searching in boardrooms, followed by late night's of strategic planning. Hence the reason for writing this book. We've been through the pain and have the scars, as have the companies who have contributed ideas and case studies, so other ISVs don't need to suffer.

There will inevitably be a level if disruption to the internal processes of the company, starting with the sales team and working back into the back office. It will change the business model and therefore the metrics used to measure the health of the business. And this will mean that the investors will need coaching and educating.

Depending on your strategy there may be a level disruption and re-education of your customers and some relationships may become strained. This is probably one of the most difficult transformations you will ever need to achieve. As our Chairman said "There is no point having a longer term plan if you can't exist long enough to benefit from it. Aim to over achieve the short term plan."

The strategic options, including 'Wait and see' are discussed in the next Chapter. But you need to make a committed decision based on a better understanding of the impact of your decisions.

Deciding not to decide is not a decision[7].

---

[7] Maybe our Chairman should add that to his list, alongside "In this market, you need to sell more than you spend".

Chapter 4

Evolution not revolution

I was a young man with uninformed ideas. I threw out queries, suggestions, wondering all the time over everything, and to my astonishment the ideas took like wildfire. People made a religion of them.

Charles Darwin (Author of the theory of evolution. 1809-1882)

YOU will be pleased to hear that few of the companies we have worked with or interviewed to write this book have torn up the rule book and started again from scratch. All have migrated to a Cloud based offering.

Each came from a different position; size, market, competition, customers and product technology. Interestingly there are a range of approaches taken by the different companies who are profiled in the case studies in the final Chapter. That is probably because they all embarked on a Cloud strategy as much as 5 years ago[8] and the market was unformed and un-informed.

---

[8] They didn't realise it was a Cloud strategy then. They just knew it was needed.

A leap into the Clouds

Lies, damned lies and marketing[9]

However the current messaging is actively discouraging established ISVs from including the Cloud in their strategic thinking. It is presented as cool, sexy, new, wacky, consumer, utility, dangerous and bleeding edge. These terms are preventing established ISVs even taking a look in detail at what it could do for them. There seem to be several myths that surround Cloud Computing, that need to be dispelled as they are counter-productive. They are:

1. Cloud applications are 100% Cloud based

2. Legacy apps with thick customer/service architectures cannot be delivered as Cloud services

3. Cloud applications are multi-tenant

4. Cloud services are billed and paid monthly

5. Cloud is the same as fog; water in a gaseous state

6. Cloud is not relevant to enterprise IT

7. Implementing Cloud solutions is faster than before

All but *one* of these statements is NOT TRUE.

A different plan

For start-ups it is simpler and far quicker, but for an existing ISV what is required is an open mind and a different plan. Many underestimate the time it is going to take migrate to the Cloud, and are already thinking about 100% Cloud based offerings as they read this Chapter.

At a minimum, to migrate your current offering to the Cloud 100% will take; 3 months to think through and agree the strategy, 3 months to define the product architecture and 6 months to rebuild. Total 12 months. Whilst you are rebuilding the application you need to develop marketing, sales collateral, pricing, pricing, select a hosting provider, and coach your existing customers.

Oh – and at the same time keep the current revenue flowing.

---

[9] And possibly also police evidence.

Strategic thinking

Firstly, you need to establish where you are in terms of architecture and commercial model in the diagram below. Then work out where your customers would like you to be.

What we've found is that many customers are uncomfortable about using Cloud Computing which is why we wrote *Think of... Buying Cloud Computing? Ask the Smart Questions*[10]. So you should really question the view that your customers are driving you to the Cloud. Don't just take the account manager's version of the truth.

The diagram above shows that the strategy should be considered along two dimensions. The horizontal is the commercial aspect. How are you charging? The vertical is how much of the solution is hosted in the Cloud. So bottom left is classic ISV 'shrink-wrapped' software. Top right is a new Web 2.0 Cloud darling. The question is how far along the arrow to Point A do different elements of your application need to be, and over what timeframe. In the interim can you go via Points B or C to satisfy customer demands?

Point B is where elements of your solution are Cloud based and is functionality driven. Point C is a charging mechanism and is driven by an OpEx vs CapEx discussion or lack of immediate budget.

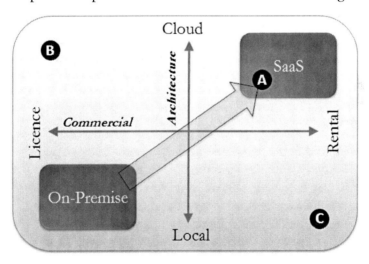

[10] Available from www.smart-questions.com

Evolve to the Cloud

Dipping your toe in the Cloud

The strategy should be driven by customer demands, tainted by the competition. Rarely are their markets where you currently operate that require a shift to a 100 % hosted service. So are their elements of your solution that would be better delivered in the Cloud – Point B?

A web-based self-service portal? A really sexy, slick lite-version that allows iPod generation users infrequent access? A power hungry reporting and analysis service? A multi-lingual front end to your database to provide global scalable access? Can you access someone else's service (data, calculation) using a web service call?

This will get you on the path to Cloud Computing. You will start to learn and over time migrate other elements of your application. At the same time you are taking your customers with you.

A pressure play

Maybe you don't have the luxury and protection in your market to move so slowly. Competitive pressures may be forcing you to move along the arrow towards Point A far more quickly. Can you take your application and move it to the Cloud using virtualization, RDP and other techniques? If you need to rebuild the application, is it a separate development team, a separate division or a separate company? The same question could be asked of sales, support and implementation.

Real life

The case studies in Chapter 10 will give you some perspectives on their route to Cloud Computing, the approach they took and what benefits they have seen. These guys were the pioneers so don't expect every story to be a straight flight to Pont A without turbulence. After all this is flying into Clouds[11]

---

[11] If you notice aircraft try and fly around Clouds. And if they don't you normally spill your drink!

Ask the right questions

When talking to ISVs of all sizes about their Cloud strategy they raised some serious questions, but mainly focused on the technology and not the wider business issues.

Naturally there is the 'band-wagon gang'. These are the ones who tacked 'e-' in front of their product during the dotcom times. Now they are simply tacking the word 'Cloud' in front of their offerings hoping to get swept up in the excitement.

What is clear is that it is not clear. There is a lack of agreement of clarity about what a Cloud really is and what the component parts are. Is it offering the product as SaaS? Is it a cheaper version of the enterprise on-premise offering? Is it outsourced infrastructure? Does Cloud require a massive ecosystem of partners? Is it a data center with APIs? What are the risks?

But you can see from the questions that these focus on the development and delivery. But there are equally taxing questions in other areas of the business. The go to market strategy is critical.

The Dos and Don'ts of the transition to Cloud Computing

Moving to the Cloud is much more than a technical product migration exercise - it will truly require a transformation of your business. It is a transition, led by Marketing and Sales in addition to your Product organization, where you will be redefining your customer segments and your customers will help you redefine your Cloud offering. The mistakes that most ISVs make during this transition are largely related to underestimating the depth of transformation required.

Extract from whitepaper titled 'The Dos and Don'ts of the transition to Cloud Computing' by Alok Misra, Principal, Navatar Group. The full whitepaper can be downloaded from *http://navatargroup.com/WhitePaper.html*

Evolution not revolution

Chapter 5

New realities

Your mind is like water. When it becomes agitated it becomes difficult to see. But if you let it settle the answer becomes clear.

Master Ugwe (Turtle, Kung Fu Panda, 2008)

ALTHOUGH there are many potential advantages of delivering your application as a service (whether Software as a Service or a hybrid such as Software plus Services), it is still a maturing delivery model and as such there are potential gotchas. Understanding these risks and controlling, or at least mitigating the risks, is critical to benefiting from the potential of Cloud Computing.

Understanding the risks

Marketplace

Despite all the hype the dominant delivery model for software is still the on-premise one. This means that there may be resistance from customers to adopt the service, preferring instead an on-premise solution. You could be too early. Or you may need to offer both a Cloud Computing service and an on-premise solution.

Sales profile and pricing

Selling a Cloud Computing service may be easier as the traditional barriers put up by IT evaporate. Customers can be up and running in hours, not months. However the large up-front license payments have been replaced by far lower annuity payments. Customer projects may now start as smaller pilots and grow over time.

Now companies such as Salesforce.com and more recently Microsoft are offering alternative service offerings, based on a 'per user per month', commodity pricing model. What will you do?

How will this affect sales compensation and therefore the motivation of your sales teams? Do you pay them when the deal is closed or as the cost of the service is recognized monthly?

Commercial arrangements

The traditional on-premise world was simple, customers paid for a perpetual license for the software and some form of optional annual 'support and maintenance' agreement. But the vast majority of the costs were up-front as part of the implementation project.

With Cloud Computing things are changing fast. The offerings are maturing and although there are some common threads, there are also many loose ends. There are different charging models varying from free or ad-funded with little or no support through to managed services with on-going annual, quarterly or monthly costs.

Product development

In a pure Cloud Computing model the service is only available when you are connected to the internet, so you may need to provide an offline capability.

The majority of IT workers in the market will be familiar with and experienced in developing software which is delivered on premise. How many of them are able to develop in the new world with the additional complexity?

And there is the two edged sword of more rapid release cycles. Whilst this is great for ensuring that new features or bug fixes can be provided to the customer more rapidly, the change from annual releases to as frequently as monthly, fundamentally changes the development cycle.

Hosting

A Cloud Computing solution needs to be hosted. There are a wide range of options. You can host it. You can find a co-locator who provides a 'home' for servers that you own, or you could run your application on a full hosting provider. Sometimes the architecture of your solution determines which options are available to you. If you have a legacy application with a proprietary database then you may not be able to use Amazon or Microsoft Azure. Instead you will be forced to own and run some of the infrastructure. Finally, do you have the skills in house and commitment to run a 24 x 7 hosting operation?

Growing customer expectations

With growing acceptance of Cloud Computing by customers, there also comes an increasing awareness and expectation about the delivered service.

Buyers are being educated about the Smart Questions they should ask[12] and this increases the requirements on you to deliver a quality service that takes into account issues such as, whether you need geo-redundancy for data centers, what legal and geopolitical issues apply to where data is stored, and the expected service Levels, especially where free services such as Hotmail/Gmail are expected to be 24/7.

iPod generation

New generations of end users are emerging from schools and colleges. They have grown up around technology that is now ubiquitous. It has driven a very different lifestyle and expectation, and many of the technologies have emerged since the year 2000:

- Everyone has a mobile phone from the age of 10. Advances in processing power, battery life, screen resolution, available systems and low cost talk plans have made it possible to use it as the universal communicator (voice, email, Instant Messaging), a media center (music, video stored or streamed), a games machine, and a micro-computer running systems.

---

[12] Consider reading *Thinking of Buying Cloud Computing? Ask the Smart Questions*

- Internet access is available in most homes so consumers have become accustomed to a very rich internet experience (Web 2.0). This has set an expectation for business systems.

- Social networking sites and MMP (massively multi-player) computer games have changed the way they interact, communicate and play with their peers. Their confidence and trust of the internet and the way they evaluate others they meet on the internet is very different from the traditional face to face meeting. They bare their souls, quirks, passions and fetishes on social networking sites, but they would never reveal them in a job interview.

- Internet search (Google, Yahoo, Microsoft), Wikipedia and a plethora of website, blogs, podcasts and video sharing sites means that information is a couple of clicks away: 'how to do something', 'where to go', 'cheapest place to buy'. It has also changed the way that they learn.

- Every one of them seems to have little white earphones permanently inserted in their ears; even when they are working, when they need to concentrate, if they are on the phone or out in a group of friends.

Technology is only technology if it was invented after you were born

An interesting insight comes from the research from Don Tapscott's book, *grown up digital*. If you grew up with a service then it is not new technology to "learn". For Generation X the TV, phone or electricity are not technology. They just use them. So, for the iPod Generation, Generation Y, the internet and mobile social networking are not technology. The iPod generation is growing up expecting to use these services, not 'learn or understand how they work'.

So should I leave well alone?

So, with this in mind, should you give Cloud Computing a wide berth? It depends. Everything we do in business (and life) carries a risk. The key is to understand the risks that we are taking, and the associated rewards, so we can make informed decisions and put the appropriate risk management strategies in place. Understanding the risks and your ability to manage them, may make a service based approach wrong for you, or it may be the answer to a maiden's prayer and resolve issues within your business. Critically however, there is a fundamental difference between risk management and risk aversion, with the later typically leading to stagnation, decay and failure.

Make informed decisions – as the Smart Questions.

Chapter

Ask the Smart Questions

If I have seen further it is by standing on the shoulders of giants.

Isaac Newton (Scientist, 1643 – 1727)

S MART Questions are about giving you valuable insights or 'the Smarts'. Normally these are only gained through years of painful and costly experience. Whether you already have a general understanding of the subject and need to take it to the next level or are starting from scratch, you need to make sure you ask the Smart Questions. We aim to short circuit that learning process, by providing the expertise of the 'giants' that Isaac Newton referred to.

Not all the questions will necessarily be new or staggeringly insightful. The value you get from the information will clearly vary. It depends on your job role and previous experience. We call this the 3Rs.

The 3 Rs

Some of the questions will be in areas where you know all the answers so they will be **Reinforced** in your mind.

You may have forgotten certain areas so the book will **Remind** you.

And other questions may be things you've never considered and will be **Revealed** to you.

How do you use Smart Questions?

The structure of the questions is set out in Chapter 7, and the questions are in Chapters 8 and 9. In the table you have the basic question, a more detailed explanation of the question and then the reason why you should care. We've also provided a helpful checkbox so that you can mark which questions are relevant to your particular situation.

A quick scan down the first column in the list of questions should give you a general feel of where you are for each question vs. the 3Rs[13].

At the highest level they are a sanity check or checklist of areas to consider. You can take them with you to meetings or use as the basis of your ITT. Just one question may save you a whole heap of cash or heartache.

In Chapter 10 we've tried to bring some of the questions to life with some real-life examples.

This is where you should find the real insights. There may be some 'aha' moments. Hopefully not too many sickening, 'head in the hands – what have we done' moments, where you've realized that you company is hopelessly exposed. If you're in that situation, then the questions will help you negotiate yourself back into control.

In this context, probably the most critical role of the questions is that they reveal risks that you hadn't considered. Risks that could seriously damage your business as we described in the opening Chapter. On the flip side they should open up your thinking to opportunities that you hadn't necessarily considered. Balancing the opportunities and the risks, and then agreeing what is realistically achievable is the key to formulating strategy.

The questions could be used in your internal operational meetings to inform or at least prompt the debate. Alternatively they could shape the discussion you have with customers and potential hosters of Cloud Computing services.

Once that strategy is set, the questions should enable you to develop costed operational plans, develop budgets or determine strategy.

---

[13] Or whether you need the For Dummies book (which we haven't written)

How to dig deeper

Need more information? Not convinced by the examples, or want ones that are more relevant to you specific situation? The Smart Questions micro-site for the book has a list of other supporting material. As this subject is moving quickly many of the links are to websites or blogs.

And of course there is a community of people who've read the book and are all at different levels of maturity who have been brought together on the Smart Questions micro-site for the book.

And finally

Please remember that these questions are NOT intended to be a prescriptive list that must be followed slavishly from beginning to end. It is also inevitable that the list of questions is not exhaustive and we are confident that with the help of the community the list of Smart Questions will grow.

If you want to rephrase a question to improve its context or have identified a question we've missed, then let us know to add to the collective knowledge.

We also understand that not all of the questions will apply to all businesses. However we encourage you to read them all as there may be a nugget of truth that can be adapted to your circumstances.

Above all we do hope that it provides a guide or a pointer to the areas that may be valuable to you and helps with the 3 Rs.

Chapter

Cloud Computing Questions

Any time, any place, anywhere.

Martini drinks advert (1970 – 1980s)

CLOUD Computing is being held up as the next wave of computing. Naturally one has to be cautious about these grand statements, however as we have discussed in earlier Chapters there does appear to be enough investment and momentum behind this wave to ensure that it is real. However it is easy to consider this as an area that requires us to think about the technical aspects. And as important as these are, first we need to consider the wider and more significant businesses aspects.

Whether adoption of the Cloud results in evolutionary or revolutionary changes within your business, there will be change. The effective management of this and the associated risks will enhance your chances of successfully incorporating the Cloud into your business strategy[14].

To help you through this journey of the 3Rs[15], the questions have been grouped into the following structure:

---

[14] Although it would be rash to suggest painless

[15] Reinforce, Remind, Reveal

Chapter 8: The Big Business Questions

The focus of this Chapter is to raise questions of a strategic nature, areas that will guide the overall approach to incorporating the Cloud into your business. These questions will be of interest to the CEO, CFO and the management team as a whole.

1. **Why Cloud Computing?** What is the business driver for delivering some or all of your solution as a Cloud Computing service?

2. **Where are the barriers to success?** There will be areas both internally and externally that if not considered could put the whole business at risk.

3. **What migration approach?** If you have existing product and services, what are your migration options?

4. **Commercial considerations** There are many business models. Which will work for you? How will you make money?

5. **What is your go-to-market strategy?** How do you drive demand and motivate your sales teams and resellers?

Chapter 9: Delivering a Cloud Computing solution

In this Chapter we get down to the details around delivery. What does your operational team need to ask themselves to ensure that they actually get an offering out of the door and in such a way that the business as a whole can sell and support it?

1. **How do you organize R&D / product development?** There are new considerations. What changes need to be made to the development team and approach?

2. **Your hosting platform.** This is a critical decision, will you do it or are you working with a 3rd party?

3. **How will your organization need to change?** Every area of your business from sales through to the back office, including the Board of Directors may be affected.

4. **What legal considerations are there?** When signing up customers, what are the legal or contractual implications?

A customer perspective

If you want to see ALL the questions that a customer could ask you, then take a look at *"Thinking of… Buying Cloud Computing? Ask the Smart Questions."*

If you are able to answer all these questions then you are in great shape, and probably in the top 1% of all Cloud Computing businesses around. So have a pat on the back[16].

---

[16] But don't risk resting on your laurels

Chapter

The Big Business Questions

Self-knowledge is the great power by which we comprehend and control our lives.

Vernon Howard (Philosopher 1918 – 1992)

CLOUD Computing is cool, current, the new thing, it is sexy. This alone has been the basis for many decisions over the centuries[17], however the outcomes have not always been those that were desired.

It is important that we remember that Cloud Computing is simply an umbrella marketing term to describe how software can be provided to your customers. Cloud Computing is not an end in itself. Its only purpose is to assist in meeting business goals or addressing challenges or issues. Therefore it is critical that you are clear about what is driving you to consider delivering your product through the Cloud. Being clear about this will inform the questions for your organization and help set a successful strategy.

So get your pencil out as you are bound to want to make notes or at least check off the questions that are relevant to your current situation.

---

[17] Especially sexy

8.1 Why Cloud Computing?

This section is all about understanding what is motivating you to consider a Cloud Computing solution. After all it is too easy to get caught up in hype of the latest 'new idea'. Be clear about these drivers or goals as they will inform your other questions.

Will Cloud Computing enable you to capture or defend a market? Is it being demanded of you by customers? Can you reduce sales cycles by side stepping barriers put up by the customer's IT department?

Maybe it is to make your offering available globally with limited support costs. Or to reduce the cost of upgrading on-premise software and drive a more agile development approach.

The way you answer the questions will vary massively based on your current situation.

- Are you a start-up with a free hand to develop the 'perfect' service?

- Or are you an established company with existing customers using an on-premise solution.

- Perhaps you have an established product, but a new powerful entrant has forced you to move to Cloud Computing.

- Has a new entrant forced you to move up-market out of your currently profitable niche which has now been commoditized?

☒	Question	Why this matters
☐	8.1.1 Have you lost business because you did not have a Cloud offering?	There is no more compelling reason to consider alternative approaches than when you are actively losing business. There is always the option to provide a solid defensive position with your customers based on your trusted relationship and explain the reasons why the Cloud may not be the right place for your sector just yet (security, data location, geo-redundancy, legislation). However if this is the right positioning for you and your sector, it would be more effective if you could present your defense as early as possible and establish the intellectual high ground For example, when the analysts are predicting
☐	8.1.2 Is there pressure from your customers to move to Cloud Computing?	Even if you have not yet lost business directly a sure sign of things to come is when your customers are talking and asking. Even if you know that the Cloud is not right for your customers yet, you should remember that the customer is always right! But you need to be ready to have the conversation.
☐	8.1.3 Are your existing competitors offering a Cloud solution?	Just as you are now thinking about the Cloud, it is likely that your competitors are as well and you need to be positioned to respond, either with your own offering or with a positive on-premise story.

☒	Question	Why this matters
☐	8.1.4 Are new ISVs entering your market with a Cloud offering?	One of the reasons for considering the Cloud is that it provides the opportunity to extend your reach either geographically or into other verticals. Unfortunately, just as this is good for you, it also means that other ISVs can extend into your markets. One of the challenges here is that you may not even be aware that these businesses exist never mind that they are competitors.
☐	8.1.5 Are the industry analysts for your sector predicting that now is the right time for the Cloud?	Arguable the first safe time to start your move to the Cloud is when the analysts for your sector are predicting the Cloud. Although you will have missed the early adopter position you will have the benefit of not having spent as much time educating your customers. As always there is a fine balance and each business will have their own style that will determine where this balance point is.
☐	8.1.6 Can you increase the barriers of entry for potential competitors?	Although the Cloud is often seen as something that is reducing barriers to entry, it may be that in your sector the reverse is true. Can you create patents that lock out or make it difficult for your competitors (or new entrants) to follow you?

☒	Question	Why this matters
☐	8.1.7 Does the Cloud present a Blue Ocean Strategy[18] opportunity?	A Blue Ocean Strategy has at its heart the notion of making your competitors strengths irrelevant by providing the customer with something so different that you change the game For example, the Nintendo Wii has been successful because it did not compete with Sony and Microsoft for the hard core gamer, but offered a console that the other 90+% of the population could enjoy. The strengths of the Playstation and Xbox were irrelevant to these new gamers. Has the Cloud the potential to do this for you?
☐	8.1.8 Will it give you competitive advantage?	Being seen as offering a Cloud offering may in itself enhance the market's perception of you. It may be part of your business model to be seen as leading edge. Any change is an opportunity to create differentiation and establish advantage in the market.
☐	8.1.9 Is your reputation based on being bleeding edge so this is just what we do?	You may have built your reputation both with customers and employees of always being on the leading edge. Working in this space creates marketing and publicity opportunities (Microsoft, Oracle, IBM et al are not that interested in promoting the use of 5 year old technologies). However depending on the size of your business you may need to be careful which of the ever growing list of Cloud horses you place your bet on.

---

[18] *Blue Ocean Strategy* by W. Chan Kim & Renee Mauborgne

☒	Question	Why this matters
☐	8.1.10 Are perceived as safe, and want to add a little edge to your offerings?	Although the marketing noise is always about the latest greatest thing, the reality is that most businesses are run on last year's technologies. Most companies are conservative by nature and hence you may have established a great reputation as the safe trusted advisor. Adding the Cloud may add an edge to your offerings, however make sure that this is based first and foremost on offering value to your customers in the safe way they expect. The fact it is Cloud is a bonus.
☐	8.1.11 Are you in a desperate place and need to do something radical?	In trouble, investors ready to close down the business, need something radical to continue. This is a tough place to be. However provided your investors and staff are clear about the risks and costs involved it may be a great way to reinvent the business[19]. The key is not to throw out all of your business experience, there are still real customers who need offerings to real issues and there needs to be sound business plan. There are the headlines about businesses that have no current revenue streams and yet have multi-million dollar valuations – remember these are NOT the norm.

---

[19] This was IMPAQ Business Solutions story, with a happy trade-sale ending

☒	Question	Why this matters
☐	8.1.12 Can you address new markets?	With the reach of the internet can you offer you solutions to geographies outside your home base? Although many of the traditional barriers to entry may be reduced, you may still need to consider partnering with local companies to provide local sales support, training or on-site consulting where required
☐	8.1.13 Can you address new industry verticals?	Can you work with a larger customer base across related industry verticals by offering multiple configurable variants on your core product? A single code base deployed via the Cloud, but configurable to meet the needs of differing verticals.
☐	8.1.14 Will the Cloud help reduce your support costs?	It maybe that many of the calls to your helpdesk are for issues that have been already been solved with more recent releases. However because the customer is on an old release and under maintenance you are obliged to help them work through the issue. If everyone was on the current release then not only would it reduce the burden on your helpdesk, it will also help stop your customers getting frustrated with the problem in the first place

☒	Question	Why this matters
☐	8.1.15 Do you need to make your solution more responsive to change?	One of the challenges with the traditional on-premise software model is that it typically works on an annual product lifecycle. This would be fine if your code had no bugs and your market sector did not change from one year to the next. However for many businesses this is not the case and whilst bugs can be addressed through service patches it may not be as simple to change business processes within a fast moving market sector. With the central managed nature of a Cloud offering and the typically more frequent release cycle there is the option to make a change and it to be available to all customers..
☐	8.1.16 Can you shorten sales cycles?	By removing the need to install your software and being able to demonstrate the production systems capability directly to the business line budget holder, without the need to IT department involvement may reduce the time to value for the customer and hence shorten the sales cycle.
☐	8.1.17 Will the Cloud make it easier for customers to purchase?	If you have flexible payment terms For example, monthly billing rather than a large upfront fee, then the budget holder may have authority to sign off the costs directly. Also being able to OpEx the costs with clear options to cease payment may reduce the concerns about lock in and budget constraints. However remember that for some businesses CapEx is still their preferred budgeting approach, so make sure you can still accept upfront cash!

☒	Question	Why this matters
☐	8.1.18 Can you reduce barriers to entry for new customers?	For new customers your mature product or pricing models may just be too complex for them. Maybe you can offer a version to provide a taste of the minimum functionality. You may consider offer this at a significantly reduced price (or even free). You can also look at free trial periods to once again get the user over the initial spend barriers.
☐	8.1.19 Can you improve time to market?	As with other items listed above the Cloud provides the opportunity to introduce new ideas and functionality to all customers at a much faster rate than the traditional on-premise model. Can you take advantage of this to bring new innovative ideas to market or to rapidly meet new legislative needs?
☐	8.1.20 Do you need to add new capability to your product?	This could either be the driver for a complete rewrite or a strategic approach to add new capability via the Cloud (where possible) to enhance the existing on-premise offering
☐	8.1.21 Have you hit barriers associated with processing power and scale?	You may have a very processing intensive part of your offering that requires large hardware capabilities to provide reasonable response times. However for most the time this infrastructure is un-used. This has created barriers both around the costs to the customer to deploy this infrastructure, but also in your ability to scale with the customer's needs. The flexible charge models for use of Cloud processing may be the right move for you.

8.2 Barriers to Success

You are happy that your motivations for incorporating Cloud Computing into your business strategy are sound and you are now fired up, enthusiastic and ready to get started.

But before we dive into the many Smart Questions that are covered in the following sections and Chapters let's start by being our own Devil's Advocate. Where are the banana skins that we could slip on? What road blocks are there that could stop us in our tracks? And are their people who could create huge inertia because they are not on board?

This section looks at this from both an internal and an external perspective and whilst we cannot possibly cover every Smart Question in this book[20] we trust that it will ignite your thought process. Additionally some of the areas covered in this section are dealt with in more detail in later sections.

---

[20] Watch out for a Smart Questions book on managing change

☒	Question	Why this matters
☐	8.2.1 Are you culturally averse to change?	Not all businesses are naturally comfortable with change. This is probably a good thing otherwise we could quickly end up in chaos! However if this is your company style then you will need to be prepared to provide greater evidence of the value Cloud Computing can bring and ensure that key players are supportive.
☐	8.2.2 Do you have an executive sponsor?	This is nothing to do with Cloud Computing, it is simply that one of the major causes of project failure is the lack of an executive sponsor. No matter how well planned things go off track and there needs to be a quick and supportive decision making process with somebody senior enough to carry it through.
☐	8.2.3 Are there key members of staff who are not supportive?	In any period of change momentum is key. A few unsupportive words or actions from a respected member of staff can create doubt or inertia. This could be anyone from the CFO through to a key developer or salesperson. It can often be a surprise to find out that these unsupportive voices are coming from some of your best staff. However they have been successful in the existing model and therefore may consider that they have the most to lose if things change.

☒	Question	Why this matters
☐	8.2.4 Do you have the financial support to bridge the cash flow change if you are moving to an annuity model?	Switching from an upfront licensing model to an annuity model may have long term benefits, however in the short term it can create a significant cash flow issue. Do your investors, CFO, accountants, market watchers understand this and are they prepared to support you?
☐	8.2.5 Do you have the financial support to invest in the new product development and go to market?	Depending on your approach to incorporating Cloud Computing into your offerings[21] there may be significant investments required. Resources required to develop the new offering, marketing to position this change in the market etc. Some of this may be possible with good old fashioned hard work and long hours, but it is so much easier if there is money to support you.
☐	8.2.6 Do you have the management skills to manage a change program	Make no mistake this is going to mean change and whether evolutionary or revolutionary it will need to be managed. This is a different skill set to managing a steady state business.
☐	8.2.7 Do you have the technical and operational skills?	You may have great staff that have all the skills required, however they will still need encouragement and training to make the most of the new opportunity. Of course this may not be the reality for you and this could mean recruitment or even making some people redundant. There will be costs associated with this and other cultural or motivational challenges.

---

[21] See section on Migrating to the Cloud

☒	Question	Why this matters
☐	8.2.8 Can your sales culture support a move to longer term rewards?	The annuity pricing used for many Cloud offerings brings the issues of sales commission and rewards sharply into focus. Sales staff who are used to the big hit of the sales bonus may find it difficult to work with longer term reward models. However one could argue that there is a general cultural shift to longer term reward models based on ongoing success and that this is something all sales teams will have to come to terms with.
☐	8.2.9 Does this project conflict with others?	This project may look great with fantastic returns and benefits. But other projects may already be in process. Can your business manage multiple projects at the same time? Does this one require resources (people and finance) that are already allocated? Ensuring that this project is aligned to others will help gain support.
☐	8.2.10 Are there legal constraints within your sector(s)?	Despite the increasing acceptance of the internet and services from the internet within both consumer and business environments there may still be legal constraints placed on the sectors that you operate in. Government customers can be especially concerned about the location of data and have included this with legal frameworks. Consider carefully whether the supposed benefits of a Cloud offering could in fact create significant customer issues.

☒	Question	Why this matters
☐	8.2.11 Do contractual obligations to existing customers create barriers to change?	Have you or your customers included contractual clauses that make using the Cloud challenging. Customer access to the physical servers (difficult in a shared facility in another country), data not going out of the country or only residing on servers you or the customer own. Your customers may even have obligations to their customers that make the use of your new offering unacceptable.
☐	8.2.12 Are your customers prepared to consider the Cloud?	You may be willing to take the leap of faith towards the Cloud, but is that the culture of your customers? This would be something to look at if you were considering the Cloud as a route to new markets/geographies where you may not have significant experience.
☐	8.2.13 Will your change create additional costs at the customer?	In isolation your new offering may save the customer money or offer a better service. But are there costs that the customer will have to incur because of this For example, new PC's or mobile phones, internal training, increase internet bandwidth etc? This may negatively change the business case for the customer.
☐	8.2.14 Is the required infrastructure available for all your customers?	In many countries the availability of high speed, low cost access to the internet is taken for granted. Is this true for where your customers operate? It may even be an issue within specific locations in an otherwise will supplied country.

8.3 Migrating to Cloud Computing

If you are a new start-up you may feel that you can skip these questions. But don't. There may be questions that you will find useful and insightful as your business matures.

If you have an established business, then this is where the really hard decisions start.

With any new idea the first thing that happens is that the supporters take a position as far away from the existing model. In the case of Cloud Computing this meant taking the model of on-premise software with perpetual licensing and turning it into hosted software with rental or annuity licensing.

Whilst this is potentially great for startups it is not so straight forward for established players. There could be a potentially large investment and may require a leap of faith to make this major shift. And so many ISVs have held a watching brief.

However the market is maturing and customer's expectations are increasing. So as always we are heading towards a hybrid world where businesses need their operations to be joined up and available whether they are on-line or off-line. This opens the door for the existing ISVs to leverage their greater maturity and enter the game – provided they can quickly learn the new rules.

☒	Question	Why this matters
☐	8.3.1　Is Cloud Computing a new product stream?	Is your Cloud solution offering new functionality not currently existing in your products? Will your existing products be able to call this new capability to enhance their existing capability, or will it be sold independently?
☐	8.3.2　Is Cloud Computing a parallel offering?	Are you building a parallel offering with essentially the same capabilities but delivered via the Cloud? How will you differentiate these similar offerings to avoid one cannibalizing the other's revenue?
☐	8.3.3　Is Cloud Computing an 'on-ramp' for on-premise solution?	Is the purpose of your Cloud offering to provide a capability that can be used to reduce the initial barrier to entry with the objectives of finding those who need/can use the full capability and will therefore upgrade to the full on-premise offering?
☐	8.3.4　Is the migration an evolution or a revolution?	Although the norm has been to develop a brand new offering based exclusively in the Cloud - a revolution - this has been a high cost/risk approach for established businesses. An alternative approach is to have a revolutionary end goal, but achieve it through a series of well planned and managed steps – an evolution. For example you might initially provide some of the existing capability as a Cloud module with no change to the license terms for existing customers. However you then provide a means for new customers to consume this module on a rental basis. Over time you add more capability to your Cloud offering.

☒	Question	Why this matters
☐	8.3.5　Can you afford to run separate businesses?	One of the challenges when offering two similar offerings is that you can create sales conflict between your products. One option is to establish a new business and brand to market and sell the Cloud offering. Although this has merits there is also the consideration of the overheads of running two businesses/brands and the potential dilution of the original businesses brand. It may of course be part of the business plan to migrate to a new brand. The key is to be clear about what the costs, benefits and risks are.
☐	8.3.6　What commitments to existing customers do you have?	Before you leap into the Cloud and bring your existing customers with you, what commitments (especially contractual) that may be inconsistent with the Cloud. Some of the key areas to check are security, data location and protection, and legal responsibilities.
☐	8.3.7　What are the internal barriers to migration?	Are there potential barriers to migration? These include staff departing, limited resources (people and money), lack of support from key people within the business, sales staff motivated to sell the existing offering over the new Cloud one.
☐	8.3.8　What are the external milestones for the migration?	Are there compelling deadlines that provide milestones to aim for? These will not only provide drivers internally, but also create compelling events that may make customers consider you new offering. For example, are there legislative changes or key changes in your sector?

☒	Question	Why this matters
☐	8.3.9　What are the external barriers to migration?	The external barriers may be a frustration that prevents you and your customers realizing the Cloud dream or they could be the basis for you to decide that now is not yet the time. It is time to establish your position with customers as a safe pair of hands. Things to consider are legal, regulatory, marketplace conditions, hosting provider capability and availability (especially geo location).

8.4 Commercial Considerations

Cloud Computing opens up a number of new business models; i.e. how you get paid. Not all of them are appropriate to your customers or solution. Any change of business model can have profound implications on the organization, motivation and compensation of both the front and back office operations.

The move to Cloud Computing also has implications on the metrics you use to judge the health and wellbeing of the company and the way you manage the finances.

With the potential for dramatically different cash flows and profit margins, getting investment for the company and managing the investor's expectations may need to be approached differently.

So, incorporating the Cloud within your business does not mean you have to adopt a monthly rental fee model. You need to ask the Smart Questions to ensure you do what is right for your customers and your own business.

This section asks the questions about:

- The cost base for delivery

- Models for recovering these costs

- Internal considerations

- External factors

☒	Question	Why this matters
☐	8.4.1 What are the opportunity costs?	If you were to do something else with the time and money associated with project would you have achieved a better return?
☐	8.4.2 What is the cost of doing nothing?	Is doing nothing an acceptable situation and if so what would this cost you? You might be trying to protect an existing product, customer base or market position that may not actually justify the costs. Although a tough call it may be better to accept the costs of getting out now and not pouring more good money after bad. Better to ask this question now than $500k down the road.
☐	8.4.3 Will there be a loss of revenue during transition?	If customers know that you are bringing a new offering to market will they delay purchasing decisions?
	8.4.4 What level of cannibalization?	There will be some customers who want to move to the Cloud service from your on-premise model for a range of reasons. This will definitely hit your short term revenue. But by how much? Have you estimated the hit correctly?
☐	8.4.5 How much will development of the new offering be?	This is more than just the hours of coding time. Include additional software costs if you are using new tools and additional hardware so you can segregate this development from existing work. Testing and documentation needs to be added and you should assume it will take longer than you expect – this is a new area of work and you will be learning as you go.

☒	Question	Why this matters
☐	8.4.6 How much will hosting services cost?	There are many options open to you in this area which are discussed in the Hosting section. However do not underestimate the costs of doing hosting properly. Do not confuse the potentially smaller costs to 'knock something up' to provide an initial proof of concept or demo facility vs a full blown scalable, high quality service. These costs can vary widely depending upon the requirements of your customers.
☐	8.4.7 What are the marketing costs for rebranding/ positioning?	You will need to invest in a communications program as part of your revised go to market strategy, which is covered in the Go To Market (GTM) section. Not only your customers, but also the industry watchers and your own staff are clear about your new positioning.
☐	8.4.8 What are the costs to provide support?	You may now be offering your products on a global basis, does this require investment in a multilingual, 24 x 7 helpdesk. Your support team may now be your primary contact point with customers. For example, customers sign up online so have no direct sales interaction and this may require new help desk skills and training.

☒	Question	Why this matters
☐	8.4.9 How will implementation services change?	Your product is already installed so the amount of infrastructure installation services is likely to be reduced. Was this a core part of your profitable revenue or was it a loss leader that you are glad to get rid of? Will customers expect to take less training and implementation support, putting your projects at risk? Just because the service is in the Cloud, the time to implement inside a customer's business hasn't changed .
	8.4.10 Are additional professional services critical to your commercial model?	For many organizations the professional services that they offer around their Cloud service are the high margin elements at the heart of their commercial models. The provision of training, business process change, integration and migration services, local onsite customer support etc. Many customers will not be green field sites or able to self educate and self provision.
☐	8.4.11 How will the new offering affect your sales costs?	This is not just about costs associated with retraining existing sales staff. You need to consider the new costs of sale such as online sign up, automated provisioning tools, credit/debit card payment etc.
☐	8.4.12 How will you handle micro billing?	If you currently have a few hundred customers with one invoice per year, how will your costs change if you have thousands of customers with invoices every month? The cost of invoicing can quickly become a significant percentage of the revenue. You may need to invest in a high volume billing solution, or work with a 3rd party.

☒	Question	Why this matters
☐	8.4.13 Are there any 3rd party or partner costs to consider?	We have already mentioned hosting costs, but there may be other 3rd parties who you decide to work with either to accelerate deployment (software partners) or for sales and marketing for the more disconnected communications with potential customers.
☐	8.4.14 What will the HR transition costs be?	It is highly likely that there will be HR implications. How much will it cost for recruitment? What will the training costs be? Don't forget redundancy costs including management time, legal costs, provision for litigation and compensation.
☐	8.4.15 What impact will service credits have on your economics and reputation?	If the service fails it is normal to offer paying customers a service credit. Free users can have all of their money back if they want! There is a balance between the cost of setting up a perfect service and the exposure to service credits and a reputational hit for a lower cost approach.
☐	8.4.16 Who will be the party that pays for your offering?	This may seem an odd question. However it may be that a 3rd party would choose to pay on behalf of the ultimate user because they would get huge benefits. An example of this is the Zanzibar eProcurement project where the Government buying departments pay for the supplier portal so that all suppliers can interact electronically with the Government for free. This reduced procurement costs. Having a 3rd party as the customer has potential benefits for you the cost of sale, billing administration and your exposure to churn is reduced.

☒	Question	Why this matters
☐	8.4.17 Does this offering need to generate revenue directly or indirectly?	Where are you going to earn your money? Is this offering intended to fully recover costs through direct sales, or is it a proxy for other services such as support, consulting and training or as a lite offering to encourage customers to your premium offering. Many companies in the open source space offer their software for free and make their money from value added services.
☐	8.4.18 Are you going to generate revenue from ad funding?	There has been a lot of noise about offering software for free and then generating revenue through advertising. Google is the obvious answer for this. A word of warning, the revenue models only really work for VERY high volume services and you also need to have the right sort of offering for adverts to work. Consider also whether your customers would want adverts directed at their users even if this meant the service was free.
☐	8.4.19 Would a Freemium pricing model work for you?	This model works on the basis that for most users the service is genuinely free, albeit at a reduced level of functionality. For most users this service will be fine. However some users will be prepared to pay for a premium service with additional capabilities, quality levels, SLA's, support etc.

☒	Question	Why this matters
☐	8.4.20 Are you going to be using a license or annuity based charging model?	The received wisdom of Cloud Computing is that you have monthly rental fees providing you with a great annuity revenue stream. And this certainly has significant long term benefits including a positive view from investors. However this is not fixed in stone and you may decide to charge for you offering as part of a traditional license fee with annual maintenance.
☐	8.4.21 What is the charge period for your service?	If you do have recurring fees, do you charge for these on a monthly, quarterly or even annual basis? This has a huge impact on the cost of back office administration and cash flow.
☐	8.4.22 Will you offer 'pay ahead' discounts?	Despite the benefits of an annuity revenue stream there is nothing like cash in the bank. So you may offer a discount for people who will pay in advance For example, pay for 11 months, get the 12th free.
☐	8.4.23 Are you going to enforce minimum contract terms?	Just because the billing is monthly does not mean that you have to allow them to leave with no notice. Mobile phone contracts are a good example of this with 12-24 month contracts.

☒	Question	Why this matters
☐	8.4.24 Do you need to include variable usage charges?	You are responsible for the costs of running the delivery infrastructure and if a customer's use of the service increases your delivery costs then you need a way to recover these. This could be part of either a license or annuity model. You also need to consider whether your usage charges are truly reflecting usage (transaction charging) or are based some reasonable approximation (organizational size, the bigger you are the more you are likely to consume).
☐	8.4.25 Are you offering a free trial period?	If this is a new approach, how can you estimate the impact? What is the likely take up and hence hosting capacity required? What are the expected conversion rates? How will you encourage take up?
☐	8.4.26 Will you charge on-off setup fees?	There may be upfront costs that you are exposed to that you want to cover from the outset. This could be services work for data migration or the purchase of specific hardware or software. On the one hand this seems to go against the 'pay as you go' Cloud model. However it is perfectly acceptable in some sectors with complex integration and data migration needs.
☐	8.4.27 Are differentiated support options a means to generate revenue?	You may wish to offer a basic support offering as part of your service For example, email and self help, with limited response time guarantees. Where customers want a more rapid response, more options to contact you etc. then this can be a premium charge. This is the model that many suppliers of open source software adopt.

☒	Question	Why this matters
☐	8.4.28 Are there any economies of scale across your offering delivery model?	Although costs will normally increase as you get more customers, you should also gain efficiencies and volume discounts that can reduce your cost per customer and hence increase your margin. How can you validate your assumptions for your business plan?
☐	8.4.29 How is your pricing compared to your current products?	Will pricing of your new offering cause conflict with your existing customers? Can you clearly articulate any pricing differences and their reasoning?
☐	8.4.30 How does your pricing compare to your competitors?	Fantastic offering, great launch planning and aggressive pricing – UNTIL you see your nearest competitor is 50% cheaper. Understand why and react accordingly. Lower margin expectations, limited infrastructure costs or cost of sale. However it may be that they have got their metrics wrong and cannot sustain the business.
☐	8.4.31 What assumptions have you made about user volumes?	The Cloud offers the chance to significantly extend your reach and hence have higher customer numbers. But what is reasonable. Be cautious of a top down approach that goes something like: There are 10 million potential customers. Surely we can get 5% of these (because 5% seems like a small number!). Therefore we will have 500,000 customers.
☐	8.4.32 What assumptions have you made for take up velocity?	But be realistic, companies who go from zero to millions of customers overnight make great headlines, but are not normal. That said you do need to have a plan for growth.
☐	8.4.33 What level of churn is acceptable?	Churn is the Achilles Heel of annuity revenue. How have you assessed the stickiness of the service and what level of churn to plan for?

☒	Question	Why this matters
☐	8.4.34 How will you handle bad debt and risk management	As you get more customers, especially where there is a self service rather than personal relationship it is likely that bad debt could increase. Also people being fraudulent in accessing your service. You need to provide for this and any processes you adopt to manage it.
☐	8.4.35 What metrics will you use to measure performance?	Depending on the models and GTM market strategies you choose, you may need to review the metrics and KPIs used to monitor the health of the business. Examples could be a shift from new sales revenue to long term revenue retention targets and to velocity of sales rather than revenue value.
☐	8.4.36 Do you need to review your accounting procedures?	Does the way you recognize revenue have to alter, or the way you book costs? How will sales bonuses be accounted for? And if you are now working across multiple geographies are there new rules and regulations that need to be considered?
☐	8.4.37 Do you establish a new legal entity or a JV for the new offering?	It may make commercial and GTM sense to separate the new offering into a different legal entity. However this will have costs associated with it.
☐	8.4.38 Do you need to accept credit/debit card payments?	With high volume, low value services the credit card may be a right approach to billing. How does this work with your existing systems? Can you create automated charges to cards etc?

☒	Question	Why this matters
☐	8.4.39 Are there tax breaks available to you?	Across the globe there are various tax breaks for businesses who are working in valued areas of technology or who are entering new markets or working with local companies. These can be a valuable source of funding especially during the early stages.
☐	8.4.40 Do your partners offer any funding support?	It may be that one of your partners is offering support either in direct funding or items that have value to you but low cost to them. For example, Microsoft's Partner Program offers free software use for partners based on the level of Partner.

8.5 What is your Go-to-Market Strategy?

Driving demand in this new market is critical. Cloud Computing may be considered an unknown and therefore a risk by some customer's senior management. Will this mean that an arm's length direct marketing and PR approach may not work?

Should you be using the book *Thinking of.. Buying Cloud Computing* book as marketing collateral to help educate your customers?

Will a more consultative approach be required, even though this seems to run counter to the high volume, low touch approach that the Cloud seems to be all about? This could result in longer sales cycles, smaller initial orders and require more experienced salespeople.

Your go to market may vary by size of company, industry vertical and geography. Are you clear about your target markets and the approach you are taking for each?

Although Cloud Computing may be perceived by many as synonymous with the low cost/free consumer oriented service with little or no support (basically clever websites) there is in reality a wide range of services available all the way up to global enterprise offerings. It is important that you are able to differentiate between these both internally and with your customers and set your pricing and value proposition accordingly.

How will you use niche marketing techniques to drive demand and differentiate your offerings in the market? Are you going to carry on with a similar approach to your customers or are you looking at a Blue Ocean Strategy?

Once you've a hot lead how are you going to service it; direct sales, resellers, partners, system integrators, online? All of the above? How is channel conflict going to play out? How does it fit with your existing go to market, if you have a current offering?

So the questions is, in this new world what is your position, how are presenting this and what is your go to market strategy?

☒	Question	Why this matters
☐	8.5.1 Which are your target markets?	Are you extending your existing markets or expanding into new ones? Are you moving into new geographies? Does the Cloud offering create opportunities in new sectors?
☐	8.5.2 How are you presenting yourself to the market?	Are you positioning yourself as bleeding edge, always looking the newest ways to help customers? Or are you safe and slow, but have now decided that the Cloud is prime time and it is time to embrace it and help your trusted customers? How does this play with your current brand positioning? If you are trying to change your style (conservative to leading edge or vice versa) how will this affect how you can use your existing collateral?
☐	8.5.3 What segmentation are you using?	In static markets segmentation often ends up as broad categorization For example, small/medium/large, number of PC's or seats etc. However in more dynamic markets you may wish to consider other segmentation. For example in the current economic climate issues such as cash poor vs cash rich or a desire for OpEx vs CapEx may talk to the desire for a Cloud service. Also the rate of growth especially geographically can indicate a need for Cloud services.
☐	8.5.4 Do you have single story for the market or variations?	Does the same positioning work for all of your target markets and customers. Do you need to vary this by industry or geography?

☒	Question	Why this matters
☐	8.5.5 How does a PEST analysis affect your GTM?	This may be an established model for assessing the buying environment, but it still offers insight to what is driving your customers buying decisions. PEST stands for Political, Economic, Social and Technical.
☐	8.5.6 How credible are you?	A challenge for any new offering is to convince potential customers that you are credible. Can you leverage your existing experience? Are current case studies valid for the new offering? Do you have early adopters who you can reference? Do you have a track record of delivering new ideas successfully? Can you get credibility by association. For example, showcased by a major partner such as IBM, Microsoft etc?
☐	8.5.7 Have you considered Blue Ocean value differentiation?	This is an approach that looks to make your competition irrelevant by redefining the market opportunity. For example the way Nintendo changed the way they looked at the gaming market with the Wii. By introducing the Wiimote they opened up gaming to the casual, non skilled gamer. For these users ease of use rather high costs graphics was the value differentiator.
☐	8.5.8 Can you learn from your direct competitors?	What are they doing? Are you leading or following. If they haven't moved why not, can you gain significant first mover advantage? If you are following can you learn from their mistakes and rather than simply duplicate their efforts can you leap frog them?

☒	Question	Why this matters
	8.5.9 Will your hosting partner / platform partner be a competitor?	What confidence do you have that your hosting partner will not offer a competitive product? As providing a competitive product on your platform providers roadmap? If not why not? If you see a business opportunity, why wouldn't they?
☐	8.5.10 Can you learn from examples in other industries?	As a high tech business the world of IT often seems to believe that it is so far ahead of everyone else that there is nothing to learn from others. Consider this position and look at other industries. The insurance sector has for years worked on the basis of small long term referral revenue. Outsourcing non-core services is normal in many sectors so why should outsourcing IT be considered new?
☐	8.5.11 Where are your potential customers talking?	Customers are increasingly using new media (online forums, communities) to both self educate and comment about their business needs and experiences. By identifying this you may be able to target messaging to specific groups.
☐	8.5.12 Can you control the conversation?	Brand protection and controlled messaging has been a key goal for most companies. However in the online world this is often not possible. You may be able to control the messaging on your own web site, or on forums where you are the moderator (although this has risks of credibility). But what about Facebook sites where people are discussing your offerings, or viral messaging via Twitter? With this you can only participate at best, assuming that you even know about it.

☒	Question	Why this matters
☐	8.5.13 What is your brand voice?	With the growing number of communication channels you will have to consider it may be helpful to establish and voice and use it consistently. Are you going to be professional but direct, humorous, serious? How does this reflect on your overall market positioning?
☐	8.5.14 What role will User Groups play?	User groups can be great for feedback and establishing yourself as credible about user engagement. However they can also create inertia by insisting that things do not change too much. Can you use an existing User Group to identify early adopters for you offering? Can they help guide the business requirements? Can they provide promotion and credibility as you come to market?
☐	8.5.15 Are your target buyers web centric?	By understanding the style of you buying community you can correctly target your messaging. Do they use the web for research, online purchasing etc? Or do they prefer a human face with physical paper contracts? Are they driven by business or technology? Offering an online, technology focused messaging and signup campaign may not be the best idea if your target customer is a traditionally minded 50 year old accountant!

☒	Question	Why this matters
☐	8.5.16 Should you consider niche marketing?	With the potentially huge audience now available to you it is important that your message is heard. The challenge is that a generic message may be applicable to all, but is of interest to none. By focusing on a niche you can ensure that you talk to their specific needs. Once you have gained success in one niche, you can approach a related niche that will value you previous experience.
☐	8.5.17 Do you go to market direct or through channels of influence?	Going direct gives you control. Channels of influence can extend your reach and provide credibility. Maybe a combination is right for you. In your home market where you have an established presence you may go direct. For new sectors or overseas linking with an established player as your channel may accelerate your growth. Going directly initially may be a way of building collateral and case studies that will be required to convince other channels to work with you.
☐	8.5.18 Will your plans create channel conflict?	If you go direct or introduce new partners will this upset your existing partners? Does the pricing for your Cloud offering undercut your other offers? If you are a startup then these problems do not exist, but for established ISVs this needs to be considered.
☐	8.5.19 Do you sell online or via direct sales?	Received wisdom would have it that Cloud offerings are sold online. However if your Cloud offering is an extension to your current on-premise offering this does not have to be true. What is right for your customers?

☒	Question	Why this matters
☐	8.5.20 Where will you get your initial case studies?	Most buyers are conservative and want to see that somebody else has already tried an offering. Early adopter evidence can be critical to mass sales. Can you use your existing customer base? Do you offer advantageous pricing to the first group of customers - may be even free.
☐	8.5.21 How do you accelerate time to value?	With on-premise solutions the customer typically buys the offering from you and then finds a way to make it work. This can require significant effort and cost and once completed creates barrier to leaving. With online offerings there is typically little upfront effort. If the user does not quickly get value from the service then there is no sunken investment cost that stops them from leaving. Time to value becomes a key metric.
☐	8.5.22 How are you positioning the future for your existing offering(s)?	If you are offering a replacement to an existing offering (even if functionally weaker initially) how will you prioritize sales vs the current offering? Can the customer base be a target for new sales or is this a cash cow that needs have its life extended?

☒	Question	Why this matters
☐	8.5.23 What will your pricing model be?	You have many choices each with their own pros and cons. Free as a lead to professional service and support revenue. Ad funded, however be careful to fully understand the HUGE volumes required to make this viable. Freemium, where the few who need your professional offering cover the costs of the free to use service. Sponsored, where there is value in one party paying for the service so that other can have it for free. And none of this stops you having a very traditional pricing model based on seats!
☐	8.5.24 Do you use rental or license fees?	Again the received wisdom is that Cloud must be monthly rental. However this does not have to be the case. Why not quarterly, or monthly pricing but pay a year in advance? Or even a traditional license fee. The challenge with a license fee can be the variable charges that you may have to cover now that you are looking after the delivery infrastructure as well as offering the software. Whilst the move to Opex is seen as positive for Cloud offerings, this does not suit all customers. Upfront payments in line with already approved annual budgets can be the right choice.

☒	Question	Why this matters
☐	8.5.25 How has the customer buying experience change for your target customers?	Traditionally your salesperson would book an appointment, listen to their needs and explain the benefits of your offering. Now the customer might be researching online, gaining experience from others, forming their own views about their requirements and the offering they need. The first thing you know is when they approach you. Provided of course that they know you have an offering for their needs.
☐	8.5.26 Do you offer specific and focused landing pages on your web site?	How quick and easy is it for potential customers to get what they want when they arrive at your site. Do they need to have links to your company history and every product you sell? They have probably already done their research and this is distracting noise. If they are here to buy then a dedicated landing page with a large 'Buy Now' button could significantly increase closure rates.
☐	8.5.27 Do you offer 'Try before you buy'?	Do this because it adds value and increases the chance of closing the deal. If your service needs some level of professional services to make it viable, then a free, self provisioned offer may actually reduce sales. Will a user be any more likely to buy if you offer them 6 months free rather than 1 month? Asking for credit card details so you can automatically start charging at the end of the free period sounds like the right thing to do. However if it puts everyone off from accepting the trial you never get the customers hooked in the first place.

☒	Question	Why this matters
☐	8.5.28 Will using online ad words be part of your marketing mix?	This is a subject in its own right and can be hugely successful or a massive waste of time, effort and money.

Chapter

9

Delivering a Cloud Computing service

However beautiful the strategy, you should occasionally look at the results.

Sir Winston Churchill (1874 - 1965)

CLOUD Computing adds whole lot of complexity when you start thinking about implementation. In the old world of on-premise software, delivery meant getting as many bug-free bits and bytes onto an installation CD. Implementation was the domain of system integrators and partners. And when they were on site they could fix any problems that cropped up.

No more. At the consumer end of Cloud Computing the only time you touch the end user it is to charge their credit card – if in fact you have a proposition that they are willing to pay for. Selling to the enterprise gives you more latitude. But you can hide less.

Whoever the customer is, you are on the hook for their uninterrupted access to the service. That means the continuous running of the application (and the software stack and database supporting it), the hardware and networking. And Cloud Computing means you potentially have an application which is delivered as a service globally from day one. Do you have the skills and resources?

9.1 How does product development change?

There are new considerations with a Cloud Computing offering. Some are benefits, such as managing only one code base and having access to it for upgrades. You don't need an elegant user-friendly installation program.

But there are downsides. Your application, ideally, needs to be multi-tenant and be able to scale massively, be ultra-stable, multi-lingual and have a really appealing and intuitive UI. So what's the problem!

Does your current application or planned application have the right technical architecture for Cloud Computing? Does that matter? You may be able to run your current application with a separate hosted installation for every customer, but at what cost?

What is your release strategy, and how do you make it easy for your customers to test the latest release? Are you going to offer configuration or customization capabilities? How are you going to plan downtime for maintenance and back-ups especially if you are offering the service 24 x 7?

☒	Question	Why this matters
☐	9.1.1 Is this a new development with no legacy?	This is the new idea, no legacy, no constraints, no existing customers pushing you one way or the other. Essentially you are a start up with the freedoms that this brings. However you also have nothing to benchmark yourself against, everything is new and there will be many unexpected hurdles to jump over. Freedom can come at a heavy price.
☐	9.1.2 Are you replacing an existing offering	Does it have to be a complete re-write or can you leave some core functionality (For example, database) and offer an updated UI? If you are writing a replacement, be aware of the challenge of customer expectations. The new service will be expected to do all the old one did only better and with more functionality. Whilst having an existing design to work with be careful not to simply replicate the old. Just because that is how it was done doesn't mean we should copy it.
☐	9.1.3 Are you extending an existing offering?	This approach potentially offers a happy middle ground. Allowing you to have a grand plan for a new offering over time (that may be nothing to do with current one) but get there through evolutionary steps. Can you build the Cloud components so they can be called by the existing offering, but also offered as a new service to customers? This may initially be a simple offering, but over time builds into a new and prime time service.
☐	9.1.4 Is your model Cloud only (SaaS) or a hybrid (S+S)?	Are you planning to offer the service exclusively from the Cloud or provide connectivity to on-premise tools? This may be connecting to your own customer or via other tools such as Excel. How does this fit into your offline capability?

☒	Question	Why this matters
☐	9.1.5 Are you incorporating 3rd party services – a mashup?	Using 3rd party services can be a quick way to provide significant capability to your service. Using Live Earth or Google Maps as a way to present geospatial reports within your offering. However the APIs for these are highly to change over time or the service may cease to be available. How do you manage testing and replacement. What happens if the service has not ceased but is less reliable than desired? Many of these services are used because they are free, this is likely to limit the amount of documentation and support. This does not make it bad to use them, just be aware.
☐	9.1.6 Are you confident that the engineering level is appropriate to the customer need?	Just because we can design and build a Rolls Royce solution does not make it the right approach. Are all parts of the service equal? Does the reporting engine need to have the same failover and redundancy as the transactional part? Do we need geo-segregated data models on day one? However it never hurts to build with flexibility in mind.
☐	9.1.7 Are you building security in from the start?	Security is one of the biggest concerns for most customers when they consider moving their data outside of their direct control. If you build security in from the beginning then life will be much easier going forward. Many of the current development environments actually facilitate safe coding by default and you need to choose to relax the rules. Think about Twitter and Facebook hacks that have been based on fairly basic attacks.

☒	Question	Why this matters
☐	9.1.8 What is your approach to standards compliance?	The obvious response is that you will be 100% compliant. This is a clearly a worthy goal, however this can quickly bring costs and compromises to performance. Consider where you are strict and where you can be less so. Areas where you need loose coupling, such as where third parties are interacting with your service, would be best kept at the highest level of compliance. Areas where you have total control and are not exposed to the user or 3rd parties may however be candidates for a relaxation of the worthy goal. The key is to always be conscious of when you are doing this and justify clearly why.
☐	9.1.9 Where are you using 'Scale Up' and where 'Scale Out'?	One of the benefits of a Cloud approach is that it offers the ability to scale to a growing customer demand. However this needs to be thought about and ideally in advance as it can have significant architectural implications later. Do you create scale by increasing the power of the single box (Scale Up), by allowing multiple clones (Scale Out) or a combination of the two? It maybe that by selecting a hosting environment such as Microsoft Azure or Amazon EC2/AWS you can let the infrastructure provider scale out for you.
☐	9.1.10 Can sections of the service be easily replaced (loosely coupled, highly cohesive)?	This is not a new idea but it is particularly relevant for the fast moving Cloud platform. 3rd party modules in your existing application may need to be re-written. Alternatively a cheaper web-service may be available that can be called. A design goal could be to create abstraction wherever possible.

☒	Question	Why this matters
☐	9.1.11 How is connectivity built in both internally and externally?	If you service is going to talk to other components of your offering or be called by 3rd parties then you need to consider how the communications will be handled. We talked about standards previously and this will help. But you also need to consider where the calls will be synchronous or asynchronous in nature. If the processes are long running do you want to tie up the communications channel, which may be lost or can you build an async process? This is also likely to be of benefit is your service utilization explodes as the requests will be queued rather than time out.
☐	9.1.12 What database architecture are you using?	This is a potentially large subject in its own right, but things to consider are: Do you have a single multi-customer model or one where each customer has their own dedicated data store (the first is arguably easier to deploy, but the second is easier to scale out) Do you use a normal SQL data model or name bag pairs driven by meta data (the first is likely to be more familiar and provides established capability, the second has been shown to offer huge scale and schema flexibility[22]) Do you assume that data will reside in a single location or will it need to be geographically dispersed?

---

[22] Salesforce

☒	Question	Why this matters
☐	9.1.13 How is redundancy handled?	Things go wrong. Hardware fails. There are many ways to provide redundancy. Some are provided natively by the deployment environment, others you need to manage yourself. Do you provide real-time, warm or DR based redundancy? Is this through a sync or async relationship and are you working across multiple locations, possibly geo dispersed? Do you take the same approach for static datasets as you do with dynamic? And what about the application platform?
☐	9.1.14 Do you need to design the service to be multi-tenant?	Cloud Computing suggest a multi-tenant application, but it is not necessarily true. For enterprise customers, a separate installation in the Cloud per customer may be acceptable. The issue is your cost of offering and maintaining the service.
☐	9.1.15 Does the service need to be multi-lingual?	The Cloud means, in theory, anyone anywhere in the world can access the application. Although many people have English as their native or second language it is dangerous to assume all people are comfortable with English. It is much easier to build language support in from the start.
☐	9.1.16 What access is provided for 3rd party developers?	Do you provide an environment and documentation that enables 3rd parties to develop or extend the application? Are 3rd parties able to customize or configure the service for customers? You may even be offering a small part of your service so it can be part of somebody else's mashup. Have you documented this and can you support it?

☒	Question	Why this matters
☐	9.1.17 Are you going to provide support for single sign-on?	Does the service allow single sign-on so that users do not have to logon twice? Whilst it may not seem a big issue, it is a major barrier to acceptance. However single sign-on has its own security challenges with customers and which approach do you take? An external service such as Open-ID or link into the customer's existing sign-on. For example, Windows AD?
☐	9.1.18 How will you offer integration with existing systems?	What existing on-premise or Cloud Computing applications do you integrate with; Oracle, SAP, Salesforce.com or custom applications. Are they plug-ins, data bridges or true integration / synchronization?
☐	9.1.19 Do you need to offer offline as well as online capability?	What is the balance between the functionality which is on-line and available offline when connectivity is lost? Do you enable local synchronized data stores? How do you handle conflict resolution?
☐	9.1.20 How is offline data security handled?	When offline, what data security functionality is provided, if the device is lost or stolen (as it inevitably will be)?
☐	9.1.21 Do you have skills in new architecture?	Does your R&D team have the architecture, security and development skills for a Cloud Computing architected product? The increasing level of understanding and expectations from customers means that the window for fixing fundamental design errors is very short.

☒	Question	Why this matters
☐	9.1.22 Do you have skills in the development environment?	Does your team have the experience in using the development tools which are needed to build a Cloud Computing product? Do you have to learn a new set of tools and languages or can you use tools that you are already familiar and skilled in? This may affect you choice of development and deployment platform.
☐	9.1.23 Should you be considering an Agile Development methodology?	Are there benefits of the shorter releases cycles possible with Cloud Computing? Are your current development approaches able to accommodate an Agile Development approach? This can be a major shift from many of your existing development methodologies and you need to think about the benefits and risks.
	9.1.24 How do you motivate your R&D teams?	Is makes most sense to put one team on the new Cloud Computing development. Possibly a new team. That means leaving the existing, loyal, team working on the boring maintenance of the legacy application. This can be massively de-motivating.
☐	9.1.25 What role does research play in your development program?	Is research a side activity that you get to when you have time, or a conscious and integral part of your whole approach? Cloud Computing is moving at pace and you will need to keep abreast of developments. Research can maintain interest and a break for hard pressed developers, can provide sales and marketing with demos that show your companies thought leadership, can provide proof of concepts in areas where you can see future demand. It requires a very conscious effort to keep time available for research; however as with many industries it can also be the source of the next area of profitable growth.

☒	Question	Why this matters
☐	9.1.26 How will new user requirements be captured and prioritized?	How will you capture and prioritize requirements? Are you prepared to use online feedback/voting and manage the expectations? The support team may be a key source of user feedback. They may be the only point of contact if customers are signing up online. There is a balance between being led by the customers and providing thought leadership.
☐	9.1.27 How will you manage the change cycle?	How do you manage the change cycle – from product roadmap strategy, user requirements, development, test and release? Can you provide traceability from user suggestion to the release in which it is implemented? This will ensure internal quality, but also offer confidence in a professional approach to your customers.
☐	9.1.28 What will you release strategy be?	Most on-premise offerings have a 6 to 12 month release cycle (or longer) with patches etc shipped between. What is your strategy for releases of the Cloud Computing service? Do you take the opportunity with the central deployment of your service to offer more response and rapid updates? Or do you tie releases into the existing on-premise product? Your sales, marketing and development teams may like smaller more frequent releases. But this is not always popular with customers if they are having to retrain every few months.
☐	9.1.29 Will customers be forced to take a new release?	Do customers have to take the latest release? If the Cloud Computing service is multi-tenant then it is available to all customers. But is there the functionality to limit new features being applied to all users? If the application is not multi-tenant what is your policy?

☒	Question	Why this matters
	9.1.30 What customization will the customer be able to do and what tools will you provide?	Do you provide customers with tools and documentation to customize the application? What limitations do you put on customization to protect the performance of the service? And how do you handle customizations when you carry out your next update to the service?
☐	9.1.31 Will you provide tools for testing and migration?	Do you provide customers with tools and a sandbox environment for testing new releases and for planning and conducting migration? Are the migration tools from competitive products or just from previous releases? How much time do you give customers to test before forcing a migration to the latest release?
☐	9.1.32 What configuration options will be available and what supporting tools?	Do you provide customers with tools and documentation to configure the application? What are the compromises made when configuring the service? Can training and help be updated to reflect the configuration changes?
☐	9.1.33 Will you offer data clean-up tools?	Cleaning customer data prior to migration is a key step for success. Do you or a 3rd party provide such tools? If so what confidence do you have that they work accurately? And how will the ensure that they are kept up to date as you change the data schema?
☐	9.1.34 Will you offer service migration tools?	What tools do you or 3rd parties provide that simplify the migration from your existing service or from a competitors. This is a critical step for customers and you will want to be confident it will work.

☒	Question	Why this matters
☐	9.1.35 What online training tools and self service support are provided?	The typically low revenue per user in the Cloud model means that you cannot afford to have the user contacting you on a regular basis. To reduce the need for customers to call the helpdesk and to increase the use of a service, you will normally provide online tools. How are these incorporated into the service? Are they context sensitive or is just a link to the online manual?
☐	9.1.36 Which devices and browsers will you support?	Which devices or browsers are supported? What level of backward capability with browsers? For mobile this gets way more complicated with a range of screen sizes, operating systems and installation programs. Being clear about your position helps, but also separating the presentation layer out provides you with some flexibility for later unforeseen needs.

9.2 Your Hosting Platform?

The selection of a hosting platform to deliver your service is one of the most important you will make. Hardware is getting cheaper and more powerful all the time and this may make you think of hosting yourself or using co-location services. However hardware is only a small part of the story. Have you calculated the true end to end cost of running the hosting infrastructure including backup, restore, disaster recovery and communications? Have you looked at the risks of running it yourself in the context of the SLAs your customers may be asking for?

You will need multiple environments, even if your application is multi-tenant. One environment for delivery, one or more for testing, and possibly one for development. Finally is there a legal, contractual or business reason for having the hosting capability duplicated in different geographical regions?

With the growing expectations of your customers, the obvious requirements such as hardware, power and cooling are only the start of provisioning a highly complex environment; the tip of the iceberg. Is running your own data center really the best use of your valuable resources?

There are many 3rd parties offering hosting services all the way from co-location through to businesses that specialize in helping ISVs move to the hosting world. For example, the SaaS Incubation Centers supported by Microsoft and independent players such as Navatar Group. We also have the emerging platform services from Amazon (EC2 and AWS), Microsoft (Azure), IBM (On-Demand), Salesforce (force.com) which offer massive provision of scalable resources.

This is a whole subject in its own right and we cannot cover everything in this section. However we hope that it will start you thinking about this very important subject.

☒	Question	Why this matters
	9.2.1 Do you a platform or a hosting partner?	A platform partner provides from the group all the way up to database and development tools. A hosting partner provides infrastructure.
	9.2.2 Long term or tactical short term?	When looking for a platform or hosting partner is the need being driven by strategic or tactical considerations? A platform player may provide a very quick route to market but at a premium cost in terms of platform licenses. But there may be a technology lock-in that prevents you migrating off to a cheaper hosting provider over time.
☐	9.2.3 Where do you need hosting capability?	Are you only ever going to be delivering your service in your local country or do you have global ambitions. Is there a benefit in working with a local hosting partner in each location you need? Or would the simplicity of a single global hosting partner be better?
☐	9.2.4 What physical security is required?	Depending on the needs of your customers you may need to deliver against extremely onerous requirements. In any case, simply turning the lights off and locking the door to the server room outside your office is no longer acceptable. 24 x 7 security, biometric entry systems, CCTV and strong physical barriers are just the start.
☐	9.2.5 How is power backup provisioned?	You cannot afford to be without power. To deliver this in such a way as to be able to offer over 99% availability is not trivial. Multiple power feeds from separate providers, backup generators that are regularly tested, with special arrangements with local fuel suppliers to ensure priority supply.

☒	Question	Why this matters
☐	9.2.6 How is connectivity to the internet provisioned?	As with power, connectivity to the internet is critical. A server on the end of an ADSL line is not the answer! Multiple providers on separate physical networks, connectivity that is as near to the core internet backbone as possible. If you are using multiple datacenters, what is the connectivity between them like?
☐	9.2.7 What level of network security is required?	Security is one of the key areas of concern for customers and it is one of the most challenging areas to manage. With the constantly changing environment of hackers and exploits this needs expert resources and expensive infrastructure solutions. For some customers this may enforce even greater requirements and potential barriers to acceptance. For example, UK Government Information Levels IL3 means you have to consider multiple border protection layers from 2 different vendors!
☐	9.2.8 What level of malware protection and scanning is required?	Files and data will enter and leave your service. Do these need to be scanned so that you and your customers are protected - they cannot introduce malware and you cannot send it out? Is this a service you provision or is it part of the platform offering?

☒	Question	Why this matters
☐	9.2.9 How is the hardware provisioned?	With virtualization the notion of you having dedicated boxes is changing. However, disks, power supplies etc fail and the underlying servers will need to be maintained and repaired. The trick is for this maintenance to be transparent to you. How quickly can additional resources be made available to you, is it dynamically provisioned from a resource pool or do you need to make formal requests for additional capacity? Although not generally an issue some customers may have approved lists of hardware, can you comply?
☐	9.2.10 What backup policies are in place?	Errors happen, data can be accidently deleted, despite best efforts servers and databases can die. Without a backup of your data you are in a dark and potentially legally compromised place. How often and what is backed up? Where is it sent? A super secure data center, that sends the backup data to a company named "We Steal Data Backup Services" may not be ideal! How quickly can it be recovered? How much is done by the platform and how much do you need to provide. For example, database backups created by you and put on tape by the hosting partner?

☒	Question	Why this matters
☐	9.2.11 How is Disaster Recovery provisioned?	What disaster recovery strategy and plans need to be in place? Although unlikely, it is possible that a disaster will occur and the data center will effectively be out of action. You need to understand what provisions have been made and what the service levels for returning to operation are. Dependent upon the nature of the services you are offering the speed of recovery may be critical. However you should be clear about the real consequences to your customer's business for a service outage as the costs grow almost exponentially as you reduce the downtime.
☐	9.2.12 What platform monitoring is available?	Prevention is better than cure, so watching and monitoring is critical. However this is not a trivial task. Internal monitoring with sophisticated tools can spot trends and fix them in advance of failure. However there are also external influences. Should you monitor CNN or Sky News to monitor external factors that may flood your service. For example, you provide information on carbon footprints for business, the Government announces a new initiative for small businesses and instantly thousands of people are finding you via Google. Matching the extra traffic to a news announcement helps to make the correct decision about how to handle the surge.
☐	9.2.13 What SLAs can your hosting platform actually deliver?	Whether you are provisioning the platform yourself or working with a 3rd party it is critical that you are clear about the SLAs both contractually and in reality. You are making contractual offers to customers about the reliability of your service, potentially with penalty clauses. You need to know if you can back-to-back this with the hosting platform's capability.

☒	Question	Why this matters
☐	9.2.14 What platform availability and SLA reporting is available?	Accurate reporting not only allows you to monitor the performance of the service, but also provide your customers with information. This is all about being professional.
☐	9.2.15 How many environments do you need?	Your service is being made available to multiple customers from the same environment. You will need to think beyond simply production. What about a shadow of production for user acceptance testing, another for your internal testing, a development environment? What about training and demonstrations, should these be done in production or in their own protected space? All of these have pros and cons with cost implications.
☐	9.2.16 Is your development toolset supported on the hosting platform?	You may decide that GreatHosting Inc is the right option for you until you realize that you need Apache web servers and they only support Microsoft IIS, or they have not endorsed the use of the latest Oracle database in their infrastructure.
☐	9.2.17 What software stacks are provided within the hosted platform?	Some hosting companies have software already provisioned on their platform that you can utilize within your service. These can range from email and ftp servers, through database services and libraries of ready to use services.
☐	9.2.18 What integration with other services is possible?	It is likely that you will need to connect to other services outside of your own. This could be through mashups with 3rd party services within the hosting platform or on the web. Integration with customers existing systems may be a requirement. How easy is this to achieve?

☒	Question	Why this matters
☐	9.2.19 What services to support ISVs are there?	Hosting partners who are focused on the ISV community will often offer additional services to simplify the transition to the Cloud. For example, high volume first line helpdesk, micro-billing services, development and migration support. These may increase the short term cost, but could accelerate your time to market, reduce risk and save money long term.
☐	9.2.20 How well aligned to customer requirements are your hosting platform plans?	A question which is hopefully obvious, however it is easy to get caught up in the pressure to provide a Rolls Royce solution when the customer may only need a Mercedes and in any case is only prepared to pay for a Ford!
☐	9.2.21 Will your hosting platform choices enhance your credibility?	If you are a large multinational business then you may never have to address a credibility or viability question. However for many ISV's this is an issue, especially if they are perceived as being inexperienced in the Cloud. A tier 1 hosting partner may help address these customer concerns.
☐	9.2.22 What are the anticipated volumes for your service?	Getting the balance right between building small (and to a cost) initially, but able to meet the expected increase in users, data volumes etc is tricky at the best of time. Factor in the random factors that could turn you into the next Twitter and Facebook overnight and it becomes black art. Building in flexibility to your platform from the outset is the key.

☒	Question	Why this matters
☐	9.2.23 Where are your customers operating?	This covers the legal and data location issues that have been mentioned elsewhere. However it also talks to latency in connections; out of China is slow, Australia to London is equally slow, London to New York is quick. Consider when overnight maintenance can be done – a 2am maintenance window in Sydney is midday peak time in the UK. Understanding your customers geographic spread will assist in selecting the correct location(s) for your datacenter(s).
☐	9.2.24 How Green is your hosting platform?	Green is a hot issue. There are the pressures from Governments to reduce carbon footprints with penalties attached. But there are also potentially sales differentiators to be had by identifying your Green credentials. This is likely to be a key selling point in many sectors.
☐	9.2.25 Where do you add value?	The range of pricing for the provision of a hosting platform is huge. You may be tempted to reduce the costs by doing some or all of it yourself. However, even though you are smart people, if you try to do things that you do not have the specialist skills for then not only will it quickly cost you more than you have saved, but you also risk destroying customer confidence and potentially the business. The key is to be honest about your core skills and focus where you add value. Do you run your own electricity distribution network, do you have a fleet of delivery vehicles or do you outsource these capital intensive areas?

☒	Question	Why this matters
☐	9.2.26 How have you modeled the hosting platform costs?	Linked to being honest about your core skills and where you add value, is the creation of a detailed and honest costing model. You need to be clear what the true costs of delivering an acceptable level of service are compared with the costs of a specialist supplier. You may be surprised.
☐	9.2.27 What are your future plans?	If you are currently selling your service in the UK to the National Health Service then a UK hosting platform will be required. However you may have established plans to grow into the public sector across the UK and then to conqueror the world. This will affect your longer term hosting needs and it may be a good idea to consider these now, even if you only execute initially in the UK.
	9.2.28 Are the commercial arrangements tied to your revenue model?	How do you tie your hosting costs to your revenue model? The worst of all worlds is paying up font for peak capacity with a 'true-up' each year. This is especially painful if you are offering free trial periods to sign-up new customers.
	9.2.29 Will they offer service credits?	The service credits are not about the money. They will never pay you enough to compensate you for the losses incurred due to the disruption of your business. They are about the hosting provider's commitment and confidence to deliver the SLAs in the contract.

9.3 How will your organization need to change?

The move to Cloud Computing will impact the entire organization. But if Cloud Computing is being offered alongside a traditional offering do you need one schizophrenic organization or two parallel organizations, or even a separate division or company?

Much of this will be driven by the Go To Market (GTM) plans you have for your Cloud Computing offering compared with those for your existing offering. The greater the difference the more likely the disruption. However although you may be able to leverage many of your existing strengths, be very careful not to simply duplicate your current GTM for your Cloud Computing offering.

Moving to Cloud Computing is no small undertaking and needs careful consideration and planning. It starts with education from the Board, investors and non-execs down. Remember – "The confused mind says 'No'".

Which companies in your sector have made the shift successfully? What can you learn from those who have failed to transition? Are there better examples in other sectors? Whilst new start-ups will have a far easier ride as they are starting with a clean sheet they still may be great examples.

☒	Question	Why this matters
☐	9.3.1 Will this affect your legal structure?	You may wish to separate the Cloud offering into a separate business, JV or brand. Or it may become an extension of your existing offerings with no organizational change. Do you have plans to exit either the existing or new Cloud business space? Will one legal structure over another simplify this in the future?
☐	9.3.2 How will internal team relationships change?	Your sales and marketing people will probably have less physical touch with customers. The development team will be working to a much more agile time frame for releases. Your support team maybe the only human contact point with the customer. These are potentially significant changes and may require a shift in organization power and even physical location. Support can provide feedback to development and become a key part of the requirements gathering process. Support may also be a major source of sales opportunities. It may allow for rapid closure of sales opportunities if the sales team are located next to support or at least have connected systems.
☐	9.3.3 What are your plans for recruitment, retention and departures?	This is a time of change and it is highly likely that you will have to hire new people, ask some to leave and worry about retaining key people who cannot see the benefits of the new plan. This will happen, don't let it catch you unawares.
☐	9.3.4 What will your partner model be?	Partnering grows in importance in the Cloud world. This is both with respect to delivery partners, hosting partner and with your sales channels. Will you sell the Cloud offering direct or via partners? If you have existing partners are they capable of selling your Cloud offering?

☒	Question	Why this matters
☐	9.3.5 Will Board meetings need to change frequency?	The business may be running to a different rhythm driven by monthly billing and regular product releases vs the focus on the annual product release and the annual chase for maintenance renewals. Does the board need to change their approach to frequency or content for meetings?
☐	9.3.6 Does your risk management culture need to change?	The increase in business rhythm is likely to require quick decision making, and a focus on risk management rather than risk avoidance. Is this something that is already in place or will it need new skills. New non-execs may be required to provide the correct oversight.
☐	9.3.7 Are new business metrics needed for the board?	Do you need to be measuring retention, percentage user penetration per customer, speed of up sell from trials? Will your top line revenue stop being a useful measure if you are receiving referral revenue rather than full value with a cost of sale deduction? Does cost of invoicing vs revenue become critical or the support cost per customer?
☐	9.3.8 How will relations with investors need to change?	Your revenue profile may change significantly. This may be perceived as good or bad, with short and long term questions. Will you need to ask for short term funding as you move to an annuity revenue stream. Your existing investors may not be comfortable with this model, but other investors may suddenly be interested in you.
☐	9.3.9 How does the marketing teams role change?	Where does marketing stop and sales start? Is marketing responsible for driving demand or only raising awareness. What support do sales teams and partners require?

☒	Question	Why this matters
☐	9.3.10 Are the accounting and other internal systems able to support the Cloud initiative?	If you are changing from a low volume, high customer touch business, to a high volume low touch one, this may have significant implications for all your internal systems. Micro billing, credit card payments, automated service provisioning tools, linked to accounts and support etc.
☐	9.3.11 What changes will be required for accounting procedures and processes?	A license or maintenance fee with revenue recognition over 12 months could be replaced by monthly invoices and immediate recognition. What about cross charges if you have different legal entities and the associated separate accounts. Do you now need to account for overseas sales, multiple currencies and differing tax regimes? Do the budgeting cycles need to change from annual to quarterly to mirror the more dynamic nature of the business?
☐	9.3.12 What changes will be required for invoicing?	Changing from a single annual high value invoice to 12 low value ones with a significantly increased customer population can create huge invoicing challenges. The cost of invoicing can quickly become a significant percentage of the invoice value.
☐	9.3.13 How will you manage cash collection?	Are you collecting Cloud Computing service revenue via credit card or invoicing and chasing for cash? Don't get stuck in the worst of all worlds – invoicing monthly and collecting cash.
☐	9.3.14 Will fraud and debt management need to be considered?	If customers can sign up online, with you having limited physical knowledge of the user, do you need to consider services that help you identify fraud or bad debt risks?
☐	9.3.15 Do you need to consider factoring?	If cash flow is an issue then it could help to consider some form of factoring to get the cash up front and let another party have the problems of cash collection, debt management etc.

☒	Question	Why this matters
☐	9.3.16 Do your current auditors have the correct skills?	Your existing auditors are excellent, but can they support you as you grow internationally, with multiple tax regimes and complex R&D funding tax credits?
☐	9.3.17 Are there tax benefits associated with your Cloud initiative?	Governments around the world are encouraging businesses to engage in research through the use of tax incentives and grant funding. It may be that the development of your Cloud offering could benefit from one of these programs.
☐	9.3.18 Do you have the correct skills to communicate your new market positioning?	Your current marketing team (whether internal or external) will have the skills to work in your current geography /industry/product. Do they have the skills if you are reaching out to new geographies, or entering new industries?
☐	9.3.19 Do you have the correct skills to talk and listen to the new audience?	You are likely to be talking to a new audience (geography, industry, business not IT). This may mean market research in different places, a new style of communication and even marketing through different mediums. The growth of community based web sites as a forum for exchanging reviews and feedback on products is huge. How do you engage in this conversation? Some of the conversation you can control (your web site, your Twitter tweets), however much of it will be out of your control. How will you manage the blog posts that criticize your service (even when incorrect)?

☒	Question	Why this matters
☐	9.3.20 Does your web site reflect your new position?	When was the last time your web site was updated? Do you have focused landing pages that allow the customer to quickly acquire the information they need, rather than have to explore all of your companies offerings first? If you are going to accept orders online can you cope, do you accept credit cards, and is the site linked to your provisioning system?
☐	9.3.21 How will yours partners make money?	Does a partner buy the Cloud offering for a discount from list and contract directly or do you contract with the customer and the partner gets a referral? Can the partner build value add on your offering and sell this?
☐	9.3.22 Will your Cloud offering cause channel conflict?	If you sell direct will this be in conflict with your existing channel? If you sell through new partners, but not all of the existing ones why not? Is the pricing for the Cloud offering disruptive to your existing products?
☐	9.3.23 Do your sales reward plans reflect the new revenue models?	The customer has signed a 3 year contract, based on monthly payments and an option to leave at any time with 3 months notice. Do you reward your sales person upfront and hope the customer stays? Do you reward as income arrives, so the sales person builds an ongoing book of commission rewards? Whilst the annuity revenue models are driving this discussion there is also a wider social desire to see people rewarded for long term success rather short term wins.

☒	Question	Why this matters
☐	9.3.24 Is your sales team able to adapt?	For some sales people the changes may be too much. Longer term incentive schemes, a need to engage with customers through different mediums and via different contact points (business rather than IT) and dealing with customers who have been able to self educate via the web. For others the change may be easy and a breath of fresh air. However as with any change do not underestimate the potential for disruption. It may be that your current top salesperson will have a lot to lose and could become one of the major roadblocks to change.
☐	9.3.25 Do you have the collateral to communicate the new Cloud offering?	Is your existing collateral for your on-premise offerings valid for the new Cloud offering? Have you focused on areas such as installation and server deployment and the customer skills needed to support it etc? What changes do you need to reflect the ready to use nature of the Cloud. Are you now selling to the business line rather than the IT department? To gain additional revenue is there a focus on training and integration services?
☐	9.3.26 Does your sales team have the tools needed to demo your offering?	Do your sales team need laptops with 3G mobile broadband so they can demo the offering? What about smart phones to show the mobile capability? Can they setup demo accounts for the customer? How do you handle low touch engagements? Can you offer web based conferences? Can the potential customer run their own demo session from your web site?

☒	Question	Why this matters
☐	9.3.27 Does your implementation team have the correct skills balance?	It is likely that a key skill has been the installation and setup of servers and software at customer sites. This will reduce significantly. Do you have the skills to now offer more training, consulting, business process change and systems integration? The money is still there, however you may have to offer different services to get it.
☐	9.3.28 Do you need overseas implementation partners?	Even with a hosted only offering it is likely that there will be services required by the customer on site (training, integration etc). If you are expanding into overseas markets do you grow your own services business to deliver this or do you look to partner with other organizations (local or global) that can offer this service and provide a margin to you?
☐	9.3.29 Do your development team have the correct resources and skills	There was a whole section of questions on this topic.
☐	9.3.30 How will you manage the changing role of support?	The support team will potentially be your only human contact with the customer (online signup). They could be an excellent source of up sell sales leads and ideas for product development. Is the support team lead involved in weekly sales planning meetings? Are they invited to development and product roadmap reviews? Is the support team motivated and rewarded for identifying these opportunities? Remember they are NOT sales people and will probably need different incentives. Support is likely to change from being a cost centre that is targeted with keeping the customer happy, to a strategic asset within the business.

☒	Question	Why this matters
☐	9.3.31 What investment is required to provide support the tools they need?	If support are going to provide sales leads and development ideas to the business how is this managed so it doesn't become a paper overhead? Do they have access to the sales tracking system? Do you implement and companywide CRM offering? Can support access the development team's product planning tools?

9.4 What legal considerations are there?

The following comments are not intended to provide any type of formal legal guidance and are certainly not exhaustive. If you have concerns regarding aspects of any contract between yourself and your customers then you should seek professional legal advice.

Disclaimer made (!), our hope is that this section will start you thinking about the Smart Questions. This should save you some time with lawyers and hopefully reduce your legal bills.

You will have existing contracts for virtually every type of customer relationship. But what changes do you need to consider with Cloud Computing? After all you are no longer providing an application on a CD with the customer responsible for the deployment and infrastructure. You are now running an element of your customer's business and hence you are assuming a far great level of responsibility and therefore risk.

☒	Question	Why this matters
☐	9.4.1 How easy is it for your customers to understand the contract?	Getting the balance right between a contract that is legally well written and one that doesn't frighten the customer away can be tricky. However you need to think carefully about how your customer sign up process may have changed. With a traditional sales engagement your salesperson could sit down with the customer, maybe involve someone from the legal team to explain any clauses etc. If your customers are now signing up online then they will only have your contract to look at. If it is overwhelming they may click cancel instead of confirm.
☐	9.4.2 When does the customer sign?	Does the customer sign a contract during a trial period or when they start production use? In both cases they will be on your service and they could impact other users. So obviously they need to sign a contract. However one of the biggest reasons for people NOT using trial software is the perceived barriers For example, credit card details and contracts.
☐	9.4.3 Do you need different contracts for trials compared with paid services?	You may wish to create some contractual relationship during a Trial period, even if very light such as 'Acceptable use' clauses. You will probably want to consider different SLA's between a free, reduced functionality and full offerings.

☒	Question	Why this matters
☐	9.4.4 How much can the contract be negotiated by each customer?	The more variations you have the greater the service management overhead so be careful about varying terms. For large enterprise sales it may be required for you to negotiate with the customer on terms and conditions. With smaller, high volume customers this may be unnecessary and too costly. Put crudely, the more money involved the greater the customer expectation for negotiation.
☐	9.4.5 Are you the single point of contract (not contact)?	A customer may wish to understand the underlying supply chain but they will not want to contract with all the separate parties. Typically a customer will want to have a simple relationship, with one party that they can hold responsible for delivery. This may create challenges or even not be possible depending on the partners you are working with. For example, Microsoft BPOS
☐	9.4.6 Can you 'Back to back' your customer commitments to your delivery partners?	In an ideal world you will only make service level commitments in your customer contracts that you can 'Back to back' with your contracts with delivery partners. However this is not always possible and you may need to take a risk based view on the business exposure this creates. This may lead you to consider insurance to cover the potential gap.

☒	Question	Why this matters
☐	9.4.7 Have you included a 'Right to vary' clause?	One of the benefits of the Cloud delivery model is that you can have more frequent releases and that all users can be on the same release. But what happens when you update an existing customer, with an existing contract to a new release with new functionality that needs revisions to the contract terms. You need to right to vary the terms.
☐	9.4.8 How will you deploy updates to contract clause?	You have included the right to vary terms, but how are you going to ensure that they are accepted. There are various options ranging from making it the customers responsibility to check for updates and their continued use of the service is deemed acceptance of the current terms, through to forcing the customer to accept revised terms before they can continue. Consider your customer engagement model and how your approach will impact this.
☐	9.4.9 Do you need a 'Right to transfer' clause?	If your plan is to sell the business when you have reached a certain critical size, then you want to ensure that it is easy for a purchaser to acquire you. If your customer base is a key asset and you don't have the right to transfer contracts to a new owner then this could increase hassle and decrease valuation.

☒	Question	Why this matters
☐	9.4.10 Are geographic variations required in your contracts?	It is normal for counties to have different legal frameworks for business and contracts. This is especially true in any emerging area where the legal framework is trying to catch up with the rapidly changing world. If you are delivering the service to customers across multiple geographies then it may be necessary to offer locally tailored contracts.
☐	9.4.11 What legal jurisdiction will apply?	Contracts have a statement about which legal frame work applies. By default you will want that to be your home country, where you have access to legal experts that you understand. However you may be delivering the service to multiple geographies and this may force you to use alternate legal jurisdictions. Be aware of the consequences in terms of costs and exposure if this is required.
☐	9.4.12 Do you need to consider insurance to cover your exposures?	Not all risks and exposures can be covered contractually. One option is to consider insuring yourself against these risks. This is especially relevant for risks that are highly unlikely to occur but if they do could be very costly.

☒	Question	Why this matters
☐	9.4.13 What SLA's are you offering to your customers?	Getting the SLA's correct is critical as they are at the very heart of provisioning of the service. Too low and your customers may not accept the service, too high and you may be paying credits too often. Are the following included; when the service is available, allowed downtime, acceptable exceptions, performance of the networks and how quickly the helpdesk will respond, how long to get the DR site up and running? These may vary by region, service type and device. When everything is working well nobody will worry about the SLAs but if things go wrong they are the key vehicle for both parties to get things resolved. Your customer will see a clear link between the SLAs you offer and the quality of your operational procedures and security policies.
☐	9.4.14 What SLA's have you agreed with your delivery partner(s)?	As a mirror to the customer SLAs you need to ensure that you have agreed at least an equivalent service level with your delivery partners. If this has not been possible to fully understand the exposure that this creates and establish a risk management/mitigation strategy. An area to watch is exclusion periods. The delivery partner will quite reasonably wish to have time available for maintenance of the delivery environment and will not want this to be part of the SLA. Consider carefully how this is defined.

☒	Question	Why this matters
☐	9.4.15 What service credits or penalty charges are offered to the customer?	In the on-premise world you can charge the customer extra for fixing their broken servers/applications. In the Cloud world it is typical for you to offer some form of credit if the service is unavailable. Consider how this varies by the service type and how you cap your credits (up to the amount they have paid). Typically you would consider excluding any consequential damage etc. However the more the customer is paying and the greater the criticality of the service, the more they will expect to negotiate in this area.
☐	9.4.16 Do you need an 'Acceptable use' clause?	People are inventive. They will find uses for your service that you never dreamed of or wanted. This may create unexpected costs or legal exposures for you. You will want to have the right to stop this by asserting that it is not acceptable use of the service.
☐	9.4.17 Should you include a 'Right to charge' clause?	Your service may be free and you have no plans to charge for it directly in the future. However as stated above people are creative and find innovative ways of using your service. This creates unexpected costs or establishes the need to higher service levels for these users. Do you ask these potentially valuable customers to leave the service under acceptable use or do you invoke a right to charge clause and engage in a pricing discussion. If the customer gains real value then this may create a new revenue stream.

☒	Question	Why this matters
☐	9.4.18 What data ownership rights are established?	Although a logical position would be that the customer owns their data there may be geographical issues associated with this. What rights do the local authorities have to look at the data or event take ownership? This is an emerging hot area and you need to be careful about what you can legally commit to.
☐	9.4.19 What access does the customer have to their data?	Access through your application is obvious. But what if the customer wants a full copy of all their data for comfort. Will this cost your support people time, effort and cost, and therefore you want to limit the number of times this can occur? Or do you charge them for the access?
☐	9.4.20 Does the customer have a right to access the datacenter?	For many Cloud models this is just not realistic due to the number of customers, the security requirement of the datacenter etc. However for large enterprise customer who is paying you significant revenues, this may be a contractual issue. Ensuring that any clauses in this area are also established in your contracts with delivery partners is key.
☐	9.4.21 What rights does the customer have with respect to DR and failure testing?	Even though for many/most customers this is irrelevant you may still wish to consider the correct notification periods and your obligations to post the results of these tests. For larger customers they may wish to be actively involved.

☒	Question	Why this matters
☐	9.4.22 Do you wish to establish an obligation for customers to support testing, failure or DR events?	Getting the customers involved with testing etc can be great feedback. For all but the largest of customers however it is probably unnecessary or even undesirable. One good reason for getting people involve is so you can say "If it doesn't work and you refused to help us with the testing, that you agreed you would do, then you cannot complain if it breaks".
☐	9.4.23 How have you structured the termination clauses?	These are essential for both parties. They need to be clear and fair. The time to negotiate, if required, is at the beginning when you are still friends. You will need to cover good leaver and bad leaver scenarios. What notification periods are reasonable? How do the parties notify each other? How much support will you offer a customer when they leave the service. For example, to extract their data, move to another service etc?
☐	9.4.24 What is the dispute management process?	It is inevitable that there will be occasions where disputes occur. You will want a well defined process that maximizes the chance of resolving this before you get involved with the courts and associated costs. This typically progresses through an internal escalation route and ideally ends at a trusted 3rd party arbitration services that both parties agree to be bound to, thus avoiding court costs.

☒	Question	Why this matters
☐	9.4.25 What 'Step in rights' are there for a 3rd party to continue service delivery?	If you are a small business or startup there may be customer concerns about your long term viability. They may be comforted by knowing that in the event of you failing that your delivery partners can step in and continue delivering the service until either they can migrate from the service, or another party takes on the service.
	9.4.26 What escrow provisions are there?	Escrow is often seen by larger customers as a comfort blanket, so that they can take on the service themselves in the event of your failure. You should consider whether this is an available option at all and if so whether it is included in the service charge or an extra charge. The terms of a customer's access to escrow and who acts as the 3rd party all need to be clearly stated if this is offered.

Chapter

10

Results, not theory

To acquire knowledge, one must study; but to acquire wisdom, one must observe.

Marilyn vos Savant (author, lecturer, playwright and listed in Guinness Book of Records under "Highest IQ")

CLOUD Computing sounds great in theory. The last Chapters of questions were valuable – but not very exciting or engaging[23]. They could hardly be described as fun. What the book is missing are some case studies which bring the Smart Questions to life.

Now life isn't always fun. Some of the stories are painful and expensive. But that makes them all the more valuable.

If we'd interspersed these stories with the questions it would have made the last Chapters too long. It would also have prevented you using the questions as checklists or aide-memoires. So we've grouped together our list of stories in this Chapter. I'm sure that you have your own stories – both positive and negative - so let us know them:

stories@Smart-Questions.com

---

[23] I struggle to think any activity which is valuable and really fun – apart from setting up and running companies.

Case study: Avalara

www.avalara.com

 Clear skies - life was fine before the Cloud

Before 2004, automated sales tax calculation and reporting was for enterprise corporations able to design and build million-dollar on-premise systems that could keep track of the thousands of variables involved in multi-state sales tax management. Small & medium sized businesses either did their best to manage their compliance obligations on their own (inaccurate and time consuming), paid CPAs/accounting firms to manage the process (still inaccurate and even more expensive), or even scarier just ignored it altogether. Most companies were unaware of the risks of inaccuracy and did not perceive much of a problem. Until, of course, they were audited.

 Clouds forming - drivers to migrate

Companies are required to calculate and collect tax on most sales transactions, so there is an obvious need to make that collection at the same time as the purchase. But real time calculation, using accurate, up to date rates and rules was always a monumental (essentially impossible) task.

But Cloud Computing enables a single provider to maintain the system and make it available 'on demand' to thousands of users. This brought real time sales tax calculation within financial reach of even the smallest of businesses.

Seeing the future potential, Rory Rawlings invented a tax calculation in 1999. He was joined by fellow entrepreneurs Scott McFarlane and Jared Vogt in 2004 and founded Avalara. The simple premise was that the Rory's 'tax engine' delivered via the internet (Jared & Scott's expertise) would revolutionize the way companies handle end to end sales tax compliance.

Cloud cover – the Cloud solution

Although it took longer than expected to find the tipping point, the trio was ultimately right. Today more and more businesses can benefit from a real-time automated sales tax solution.

Continuing technological advances have raised speed, reliability and availability, but the key for Avalara was harnessing that power into the financial, POS and ecommerce applications companies use to track their businesses. Today, users of QuickBooks, Microsoft Great Plains, or any of more than 80 other accounting/ERP programs simply enter an address and a sales amount into their application and Avalara's AvaTax service returns a precise, up-to-date sales tax amount in less than a second. The transaction record is stored for accurate reporting and remittance to any of the nation's 14,000+ taxing jurisdictions. For Avalara, software-plus-services truly is the only business model that solved the customers problems—the only way to take an automated sales tax solution to market.

 ## Sunny spells - the benefits

In the past, the only choice most companies had for managing their sales tax compliance obligations was manual calculation, which took massive amounts of time and could not be trusted for complete accuracy. Research on constantly changing jurisdictions, rates, taxability rules, and other requirements could be a full time job, or more. And applying the rates for the right jurisdictions in real time as transactions occurred was next to impossible.

A centralized system delivered via the Cloud is cheaper, more accurate, and constantly aligned with the tax jurisdictions. Combine this with the simple, seamless integration to financial systems, ERP, and e-commerce and it is compelling for an SME.

But now even massive enterprises are wondering about the value of making the internal investment in the light of fast, accurate and extremely affordable Cloud-driven solutions.

Case study: CODA

We have been impressed by what CODA has achieved in such a short space of time.

Jason Cremins, CEO of Remote Media

www.coda2go.com

 ## Clear skies - life was fine before the Cloud

CODA has been experts in on-premise finance for 28 years with customers operating across 100 countries. Their financial accounting software has a formidable reputation, and resides on local servers in some 2,600 mid-to-large organizations around the world.

"We have a 'multi-everything' approach: multi-lingual, multi-currency, multi-company. In the accounting world, we enjoy enormous credibility, especially among mid- to enterprise-level organizations," said Liz Schofield, CODA's group marketing manager.

 ## Clouds forming - drivers to migrate

"On-demand solutions are not only growing in popularity, but—as Salesforce.com has proven—can have broad market penetration," said Schofield. "It became clear to us that we needed to be on an on-demand platform, and that ultimately meant building on Force.com."

"Software as a Service is a logical extension of CODA's 'open platform' commitment. Delivering CODA 2go on the Force.com platform will allow CODA to offer our product portfolio to a far wider range of businesses," said Jeremy Roche, CEO of CODA.

CODA's development team had been reviewing the emerging market for on-demand applications for some time, but the CODA 2go project was prompted by repeated customer requests to integrate Salesforce's CRM with CODA's accounting applications.

Cloud cover – the Cloud solution

The service branded CODA 2go delivers CODA's award-winning 'multi-everything' finance functionality organizations of all types and sizes, hosted as an on-demand service. It is the first enterprise-level application to be designed, built and delivered on the same, single platform of Force.com.

CODA 2go debuted with sales invoicing and accounts receivable functionality, addressing a clear demand from many organizations for a seamless, software-as-a-service solution to manage the process of converting orders into cash.

The innovation is far from over. CODA has now delivered accounts payable and full general ledger functionality. It is looking to other areas such as procurement, assets, and sales order processing.

"We have planned a full roadmap based on our experience in the market, the appearance of additional functionality will in part depend on where our early adopters push us," Schofield says.

 ## Sunny spells - the benefits

The project at first seemed daunting. "We knew that developing our own on-demand platform in-house would be a lengthy and expensive project and that we were looking at least two years before we could start building the solution on the platform," says Schofield. "Even with Force.com, we initially thought that development would be difficult and time consuming, but we were quickly proven wrong.

"CODA 2go is simple to set up and use and cost-effective to run, and for many companies and subsidiaries, it will better meet their accounting requirements than on-premises software," said Jeremy Roche, CEO of CODA. "We expect it to quickly become the de facto Cloud accounting solution for Salesforce.com customers, as well as those companies that are looking for an on-demand accounting application that is more sophisticated than others on the market, without the complexity and cost that often implies."

Case study: Jobscience

TalentCentral is unique in that it was designed directly in response to small-business need, but can be used in any sized company. It can be up and running in an afternoon, works seamlessly with current applications, and is totally customizable.

Ted Elliott, CEO of Jobscience

www.jobscience.com

 Clouds forming - driver to develop

A longtime Salesforce.com customer, Elliott was an early supporter of Cloud Computing, visualizing not only the benefits for his company's operations, but also how the company could adapt its business model to better meet its customers' needs via the Cloud.

Jobscience's first Force.com-based product came about almost by accident. The company was asked to create a version of its recruiting system for Hire Heroes, an initiative of the Health Careers Foundation. The organization specializes in career placement for servicemen that have been wounded or disabled.

Elliott quickly determined that the best and most efficient way to deliver a high-quality hiring system was to leverage the Cloud. Based on the enthusiastic response of the organization, Elliott decided that his company should pursue a new business opportunity developing applications based on the Force.com platform.

 Cloud cover – the Cloud solution

Jobscience started by building an on-demand application to automate all aspects of a company's recruiting process. They now offers a full suite of talent management products including TalentStaffing for finding and hiring the best recruits, TalentCentral for creating and managing a company's career portal, and TalentPlan for adapting staffing plans to fulfill a company's corporate mission.

They've just launched a first of its kind, cost-effective applicant tracking system for only $1/user/month. It combines any edition of Salesforce.com CRM with an Enterprise account of Google Apps to give staffing companies and HR departments strapped by todays economic conditions an affordable, functional tool that introduces them to Cloud Computing.

 ## Sunny spells - the benefits

Force.com offers all of the power of .NET and J2EE without the worries of building and maintaining the infrastructure needed to provide on-demand solutions based on those platforms. Jobscience doesn't need to invest in hardware and software to deliver its products, or in the manpower needed to maintain them. Elliott estimates that the company is saving at least $40-50,000 each month by outsourcing the infrastructure. "Not only is it cheaper," he points out, "It is also more reliable."

Another key advantage of working with Force.com is the ability to quickly iterate so products can be constantly improved. "When we started working with Force.com we couldn't believe the difference," says Elliott. "Working with other technologies it would have taken ten times the amount of resources and effort. Now we can build new features and products in days or weeks. We can do prototypes virtually overnight." New products and versions can be made available over the AppExchange, swiftly reaching an appreciative audience.

As the market penetration of Cloud Computing tools grows, the opportunities for Jobscience will continue to skyrocket. By basing its development efforts on the Force.com platform, the company can continue to stay ahead of the competition with faster dev cycles, lower infrastructure costs, and the ability to leverage Salesforce.com's own development efforts.

For Jobscience, the future is anything but cloudy.

Case study: Linden Lab

CloudFront has significantly reduced the time it takes for our Residents to download our Viewer, wherever they are. The process for getting up and running with CloudFront was simple and straightforward, and took just a few minutes.

Bryan O'Sullivan, Linden Labs

www.lindenlab.com

 Clear skies - life was fine before the Cloud

Linden Lab is the maker of Second Life, the immersive 3D virtual world imagined and created by its users or Residents. Since 2006, Linden Lab has used Amazon Simple Storage Service (Amazon S3) to store elements used in the Second Life world and to distribute the Second Life Viewer to end users.

 Clouds forming - drivers to migrate

In November 2008, when AWS released Amazon CloudFront, a content delivery service, Linden was faced with a decision: which service should it use to deliver its content?

 Cloud cover – the Cloud solution

Perhaps not surprisingly, the right answer for Linden Lab was to use both services. They decided to use CloudFront for some of their content, while other content remained only in Amazon S3.

They made the determination based on the popularity of their content: those objects that were downloaded frequently would be moved to CloudFront, those that were downloaded less frequently would be delivered through Amazon S3 alone.

Specifically, Linden Lab first enabled a CloudFront distribution for downloads of the Second Life Viewer. The Second Life Viewer is an application that each Resident runs on their own computer to interact with the Second Life world. Downloads of the Viewer were ideally suited for CloudFront delivery.

The Viewer can be downloaded over 40 thousand times each day by different users all over the world and using CloudFront helps Residents download their software faster by storing copies at edge locations close to them. Currently, CloudFront uses 14 edge locations across the world.

At the same time, Linden continues to use Amazon S3 for its less frequently accessed content, particularly assets used as part of the Second Life in-world experience. These include assets like sounds, skeleton and texture files, and animations that are part of every Resident's inventory.

Next, Linden Lab plans to enable map tiles for delivery with Amazon CloudFront. Second Life Residents can use map tiles to navigate and travel in the online world. So, like the Second Life Viewer, individual map tiles are popular objects that are well suited for CloudFront's edge delivery: each map tile is requested many times by users all over the world.

 ## Sunny spells - the benefits

With CloudFront, copies of map tiles will be held in edge locations close to Viewers, reducing latency and improving the user experience.

"We chose to store our less frequently accessed content in Amazon S3 because it gives high durability for great value," said O'Sullivan.

Case study: Navatar Group

Navatar's SaasCase™ is designed to help software companies fully understand the business impact of moving to SaaS delivery on the Force.com platform by giving them a clear set of cost and benefit expectations.

NAVATAR
GROUP

www.navatargroup.com
blog - www.navatarforce.com

Clarence So, Chief Marketing Officer, Salesforce.com

 Clouds forming - drivers to migrate

The Navatar founders, Deloitte Consulting veterans, had years of experience developing CRM and technology solutions for large Financial Services firms. In 2004 they quickly saw the potential for SaaS and became early partners with Salesforce.com. The Wall Street office was established to bring enterprise level, affordable CRM services to the SMB financial market.

True Cloud Architecture arrived in 2007 with Force.com and Salesforce.com commissioned Navatar as an OEM partner to build and market products for the Financial Sector. As Navatar started building products on Force.com, they quickly learned some important lessons.

- the Cloud model provided Navatar access to the entire global market, dramatically extending its reach - a larger market segment requiring more salespeople.

- SaaS offering meant lower upfront payments – cash flow had to be carefully managed.

- a Cloud service meant establishing a continuous relationship with each customer – more investment in customer support and success.

It became clear that the Cloud products would also require a different business model.

Cloud cover – the Cloud solution

The Navatar Product Engineering team was established in 2007 and Navatar Private Equity for Salesforce.com was launched in 2008. Salesforce.com's powerful marketing team helped spread the word – the Wall Street world was beginning to intersect with Cloud Computing. Early customers started to help Navatar enhance the product with more advanced features beyond CRM, such as Deal Management, Capital Calls and Investor Reporting. An early vertical products on a Cloud platform was taking shape.

The customer base started growing and Navatar started working on the other parts of the transition. Product sales and support teams were created in the New Delhi office. Today, Navatar's product sales, product management and product support teams manage 80% of all the sales, product management and support, out of their New Delhi office, supporting customers worldwide.

On-Premise firms started noticing Navatar's success and were looking to migrate their products to the Cloud and needed advice and help. As Navatar started helping other ISVs build their commercial products on Force.com, a new practice to help ISVs build, launch, sell and support their products was created.

Starting with a Proof-Of-Concept and a Business Case, the Cloud Services program is designed to help an ISV develop a Cloud product, as well as provide an offshore India-based ready product, sales and support teams for ongoing operations.

 ## Sunny spells - the benefits

In less than two years, Navatar has become the leading provider of Salesforce-based products for the Financial sector, challenging the larger, established ISVs. Navatar's customers can now get a version of Salesforce that fits their needs out-of-the-box. That means no implementation costs, no maintenance costs and no support costs for a firm – it's all done for a low monthly subscription fee.

A user within Alternative Investments can get going with an application completely customized to manage prospective investors, investor relations, fundraising, deal flow, investments and fund portfolio, for a daily cost as little as the price of a coffee!

Case study: Nimbus

We've been staggered by how successful our Software plus Services strategy has been. And how (relatively) painless to implement.

NIMBUS
from strategy to reality

Adrian King, COO

www.nimbuspartners.com

 Clear skies - life was fine before the Cloud

In business, change is often difficult to accommodate throughout the organization. Especially for large organizations, adapting to satisfy new regulations, merging with or acquiring companies, striving to drive efficiencies or perform better, or implementing IT software.

Since 1997 Nimbus has been delivering software that delivers that process-focused content as an Intelligent Operations Manual to every employee via the web or mobile devices. It enables companies to measure and gain visibility of end to end processes, define each individual's role, responsibility and accountability and align day to day actions with corporate strategy.

Nimbus Control 2007 is developed on Microsoft technologies and integrates into core IT systems such as ERP, document management, BI and email.

 Clouds forming - drivers to migrate

Nimbus sold on-premise software licenses and provided implementation consulting services. Nimbus was faced with long sales cycle and frequent roadblocks by customers' IT departments due workload or server capacity, customer's outsourced IT providers, or the perceived risk of deploying Nimbus' solution broadly. "When a major investment bank said it would take nine months to install a server for the project, we knew we needed to find a way for prospective customers to realize the business benefits of our solution," said Richard Parker, Founder and EVP Global Sales.

Cloud cover – the Cloud solution

By offering to host the Control 2007 solution, Nimbus could make it possible for the customer project to be launched immediately. Nimbus opted to put the hosted environment in a co-location facility as they were providing their legacy application a service, and therefore it was not architected to use infrastructure service such as Microsoft Azure. By hosting they reduced the lead time for getting the solution operational from months or weeks to just 24 hours.

This was the start Nimbus' use of the software-plus-services business model. The hybrid business model, allows customers run proof-of-concept and early stage projects for and gives an IT department time to validate the solution and prepare the company's infrastructure to support it internally.

"The target is not to host Control 2007 long term for customers, although we do in some cases, but to allow customers to launch business change projects quickly using our solution," said Parker.

 ## Sunny spells - the benefits

Nimbus now provides hosted, on-premise, and hybrid implementations of its solution. The transition to a hybrid business model has resulted in:

- Exceptional revenue growth. Revenue grew 48%, 52% and 39% in the last 3 years, as compared to 5% annual growth before the Cloud strategy was implemented.

- Shorter sales cycle. On average, sales cycles were reduced by 3-6 months because business decision makers can sign up for (and expense) Nimbus's solution instead of going through their IT departments. If they like the solution and want to roll it out broadly, they can continue to have it hosted or migrate it in-house.

- Happier field employees. With IT hardware and software hosted by Nimbus, there's better control of the infrastructure. Field professionals at Nimbus can access and trouble-shoot from anywhere, which decreases travel time and employee burn-out.

Case study: NitroSell

Our solution is market- disruptive. We offer enterprise class software at SMB prices, so the ROI is measured in months not years.

Tom Keane, President

www.nitrosell.com

 Clouds forming - drivers to migrate

NitroSell is VC backed and was founded in 2005 to deliver enterprise class eCommerce at an SMB price point to a global market of retailers. To achieve this goal, the company had to deliver a price point dramatically below the current threshold for such systems and hide all technical complexity from the target customer base, which typically doesn't have an IT department. NitroSell also had to find and leverage a virtual sales network with an existing presence in NitroSell's target customer base, and support those sales partners using an efficient one-to-many model. Migrating to the Cloud was the natural choice.

 Cloud cover – the Cloud solution

NitroSell enables small-to-midsize brick-and-mortar retailers to increase sales and profits by implementing and running integrated online stores, no matter where in the world they are based. When NitroSell e-Commerce is used with on-premise Microsoft Dynamics, the result is a single, integrated multi-channel sales solution for managing both in-store and online sales channels.

NitroSell combines their eCommerce Cloud solution with the power, stability and features of the in-store Microsoft Dynamics software which is installed on-premise. NitroSell web-enables Dynamics in clever and sophisticated ways, but this is entirely hidden from the end-user retailers, who experience a quick-to-install, highly customizable, easy-to-operate multi-channel sales system.

NitroSell's approach means the retailer also benefits from their Cloud services for provisioning, support, and billing, which further reduces the initial and ongoing costs of the system. This approach means NitroSell can deliver more sophisticated systems to a larger retailer user-base (global in nature) at a lower cost which is charged monthly as a service. NitroSell will ultimately implement and support a mass-market number of systems so has developed a web-based customer and partner portal and billing system. This portal provides self-service facilities to NitroSell's Microsoft Dynamics partners, who in turn can use it to service their retail customers.

 ## Sunny spells - the benefits

Adapting a Cloud model and delivering solutions co-operatively with Microsoft Partners has enabled NitroSell to deliver enterprise-level multi-channel benefits and functionality at a small business price, right across the globe.

NitroSell's customer base is highly diverse by size, sector and geography. It has now reached critical mass with revenues growing exponentially, and monthly service fees now delivering 70% of Nitrosell's revenues.

The benefits of a Cloud business model have resulted in:

- *Rapid Market Traction.* NitroSell has web-enabled more than 1400 retail businesses in 10 countries in less than 4 years. More than 2.7m customers have online accounts on NitroSell's customer web stores.

- *Highly competitive pricing and compelling ROI.* By investing in a robust back-end billing and provisioning system and recouping costs from subscription revenue, NitroSell can deliver a solution at a lower price point that the competition; typically less than 3% of their direct online revenues, so ROI is measured in months, not years.

Case study: David Kroenke & NSPI

My students don't want to buy a book, so why do I insist on selling them one?

David Kroenke, Author   *www.QuadraLearningSystems.com*

As businesses are learning to appreciate the value of outsourcing, software plus services is quickly gaining traction.

Stephen Moss, COO, NSPI   *www.nspi.com*

 ### Clear skies - life was fine before the Cloud

When award winning author David Kroenke wrote the first edition of his MIS books, the process of publishing and selling textbooks to higher education institutions was mature, well-known and established - almost to the point of a time honored tradition.

"We enjoyed 90 percent plus sell through. If the class had 100 students, we might sell 95 books," mused Kroenke, wistfully. "Yes, there were some used books on the market, even then, but they weren't a significant factor."

 ### Clouds forming - drivers to migrate

Until the late 90's, Kroenke and Pearson Publishing focused on delivering traditional textbooks to an expanding international audience. Publishers, professors and students understood this model, but when internet-based used book vendors gained momentum, the sale of used textbooks cut dramatically into publisher sales revenue. "You earn revenue for about one semester, and that's it," according to Kroenke.

On top of the used-book challenge, student preferences began to change. Increasingly students wanted more dynamic and interactive content, content that more closely resembled their early-year experiences with educational television. It became clear that future success depended on delivering dynamic content, online, using a licensing model.

Cloud cover – the Cloud solution

"Research on student learning styles indicates that the majority of students want to actively engage with educational materials," says Kroenke. "At the same time, however, the economics of publishing make it cost infeasible to hire a Flash programmer for every lesson. Hence, I looked for new and emerging technologies that would enable me to quickly and inexpensively create interactive, web-based programs, delivered over the Cloud."

NSPI worked with Kroenke and Pearson Publishing and, in 2008, utilized Microsoft Sharepoint technologies to provide collaborative experiences to 12,000 students at more than 100 universities. Within a year, this software-plus-services approach enabled David to drive content directly to the learner's computer and develop collaborative connections directly with those using his texts.

Working with NSPI, in 2009 Kroenke successfully launched Quadra™ and the next generation educational experience. Quadra™ lessons employ Microsoft Silverlight to present educational content via animation, dynamic graphics, audio, video, Deep Zoom, and innovative practice games that re-enforce the students' learning. Behind the scenes, Quadra™ records student activity in SQL databases and then publishes reports of student activity to professors.

NSPI is a Microsoft Gold Certified Partner that hosts and manages infrastructure fabric of the Quadra™ solution. Kroenke said that he chose NSPI because of the high quality performance, security, and reliability that he and his textbook customers experienced with NSPI's SharePoint solution. Also, NSPI's experience with Microsoft technologies was crucial to Quadra™ implementation; including servers, facilities and complete backup and disaster recovery.

 ## Sunny spells - the benefits

"The marriage of NSPI's cloud, leading edge Microsoft products, and Quadra™ technologies enables non-programmer content experts to create and deliver innovative content, at a fraction of the cost of past technologies like Flash," according to Kroenke.

Case study: SMBLive & Mural Consulting

SMBLive has balanced rapidly changing customer needs and evolving technologies to deliver cloud-based services that help small businesses get found online, engage with customers, and sell more.

Matt Howard, CEO, SMBLive   *www.smblive.com*

SMBLive was willing to make the cloud-based technology investments required to continue to demystify the web for their small business customers.

Jeff Hagins, Partner/CTO, Mural Consulting   *www.muralconsulting.com*

 ### Clouds forming – driver to develop

SMBLive was founded in 2005 to build SaaS applications for small businesses. Mural Consulting helped with their overall product and go-to-market strategy and supported SMBLive as they embarked on a strategy of helping small businesses to engage customers online. For many small businesses, online is new territory, and they need a partner to help make it simple.

The first version of SMBLive's flagship product was built and launched in partnership with a Tier-1 Telecom provider. Within 12 months of the production launch of the offering, they had 300,000 customers and climbing! Things should have been great; however like many early stage SaaS businesses, they discovered their costs were still too high compared to revenue. SMBLive offered a 'Freemium' class of service, and scaling the offering to support hundreds of thousands, even millions of customers, was a challenge in terms of operational costs. Their solution was architected to accommodate the peak daily load for the service, so they were paying for infrastructure that was being used to support a peak operational requirement during just two hours of each day.

The large number of servers and a lack of automation with respect to server deployment was driving high costs both for hosting and operations/support labor. The result was a focus on operational priorities that was keeping the business from adding the next generation of features and functionality the SMB community needed.

Cloud cover – the Cloud solution

Mural guided SMBLive through a complete re-engineering of their solution to run in the Amazon Cloud using various Amazon Cloud Computing services such as EC2, S3 and SQS. The entire re-engineering effort was accomplished in 12 weeks and the result has been a reduction in operational costs of nearly 70% compared to the previous architecture. Both hosting and labor costs have been significantly reduced. In addition, while Mural and SMBLive were re-engineering the solution, they took advantage of the opportunity to assess the solution against current small business requirements and realized that the current solution was not keeping pace with the changing landscape of social media and increasingly web-centric consumer behavior. Mural helped SMBLive to identify, design, and develop a whole new suite of capabilities for allowing small businesses to engage customers online.

 ## Sunny spells - the benefits

With Mural Consulting's support, SMBLive has been able to stay current with the rapidly evolving landscape of internet marketing trends. They deliver a solution to small businesses to help them grow their business by engaging their customers online throughout the entire web-centric customer lifecycle.

In addition, the shift from traditional hosting to utility computing infrastructure has meant a change from an operational to a more strategic focus. This has helped them to focus on growing their business through new channel partner relationships instead of focusing exclusively on how to service the existing relationships.

Mural's expertise across all areas of Cloud Development (including Business/Financial Management, Application Architecture, Hosting Architecture, Operations/Support, and Go-To-market Best Practices) meant that they could take a holistic view of SMBLive and help them redefine their business to take advantage of the latest industry developments instead of being threatened by them.

Case study: Thomas International

We believe that that the way in which Thomas delivers its products is just as important the products themselves. Ease of access has and will continue to be critical to our success.

www.thomasinternational.net

Martin Reed, Chairman, Thomas International

 ## Clear skies - life was fine before the Cloud

With a presence in 60 countries, Thomas is one of only a handful of truly global providers of on-demand behavioral and aptitude assessments. Since the Thomas Personal Profile Analysis (PPA) was first launched, it has migrated from pen and paper (1972), to on-premise desktop software (1988 & 1996), to a full ASP solution (1999).

 ## Clouds forming - driver to develop

"It's obvious that the pace of technological change is increasing, not decreasing" said Martin Reed, Thomas' Chairman. "What hasn't changed is Thomas' commitment to the belief that: Increased Accessibility = Increased Consumption."

In the business of recruiting and team building, increased accessibility means ease of access for administrators and ease of access for candidates. Simply put, the easier you make it for administrators and candidates to consume your product, the more they'll consume.

 ## Cloud cover – the Cloud solution

By 2007, Thomas boasted one of the most powerful web portals in the assessment industry handling over 90% of the one million plus Thomas assessments completed each year. Yet Thomas came to the realization that it could no longer be an island and took a decision to begin focusing on application portability - the ability to quickly and economically integrate its assessment functionality onto a variety of distribution partner platforms, ecosystems and application suites.

Some clients had already begun demanding that Thomas tools be made available on other HR platforms. A Canadian client made the availability of the Thomas PPA a pre-condition for its migration to Taleo's Business Edition. The result is that today Thomas and Taleo offer an integrated solution that includes client-branded career websites and an array of assessment tools that empower employers to better recruit and retain active as well as passive candidates.

In migrating to an on-demand delivery model, many independent software vendors attempt to provide clients with their entire range of products. The logic being, the more robust the offering, the more impressed the client will be. In fact, Thomas found the opposite to be true. Less is more. To be successful they withheld significant portions of their functionality, essentially simplifying the product. This enabled clients to be self sufficient in using the application. The result has been less customer support and greater scalability.

 Sunny spells - the benefits

Today clients can access Thomas' behavioral and aptitude assessment tools and training by working with over 300 certified Thomas Sales Consultants. But what about clients who wish to access Thomas in a self-serve capacity - i.e. a frictionless store-front. This is a group of customers Thomas spends a lot of time thinking about.

Contrary to the strategies of some SaaS or on-demand providers, Thomas' goal in store-fronting would not be the disintermediation of its sales consultants. Thomas' consultants have been and will remain key to the Company's competitive advantage.

However, application self-sufficiency equals true scalability. There are clients who will be inclined to find, evaluate and ultimately purchase Thomas products without ever speaking to a Sales Consultant. These are small to medium enterprises, although larger enterprise-level organizations will likely follow suit, eventually. Addressing this need will require further change in Thomas distribution model. Fortunately, change is nothing new to Thomas.

Case study: TriSys

With TriSys ASP, our customers can eliminate the cost of replacing servers, upgrading software licenses, ... and maintaining IT headcount—all of which adds up to significant ongoing savings.

Garry Lowther, CEO

www.trisys.biz

 ### Clear skies - life was fine before the Cloud

When TriSys first emerged in the early 1990s, the process of soliciting and reviewing resumes or CVs - and then matching prospective candidates to open positions - was a manual, time-consuming task.

The early versions of the product solved this challenge by integrating free text searching with database searching so that recruiters could say, 'I want someone who's available by this date, wants to work in this location, and lives within a 20-mile radius of this particular city.' Before TriSys, recruiters simply couldn't perform this type of multiple query search.

 ### Clouds forming - drivers to migrate

During its first decade in business, TriSys delivered its solutions using the traditional on-premise deployment model. This delivery method worked well for large recruitment agencies with the budget to maintain onsite IT infrastructures. But as the work of recruiting became more automated, many small agencies could not afford to maintain their own servers and IT personnel.

Getting started as a one-person operation is relatively simple and affordable - all a new recruiter needs are a few customers, a stack of resumes, a phone, and a computer. But what happens when a home-based recruitment agency decides to expand? How can an independent recruiter scale to meet the needs of an ever-increasing customer base while still retaining the flexibility and cost efficiencies of a home-based business?

Cloud cover – the Cloud solution

To address these questions, TriSys looked beyond the traditional on-premise deployment model to develop hosted and combined (or hybrid) delivery options. "We started thinking about providing a low-cost virtual office environment for start-up recruitment companies," says Lowther. "If we could develop a solution that gave these home-based businesses virtual access to the infrastructure that one would normally find in an office environment, then they could grow their businesses while continuing to work from home."

TriSys developed an on-demand delivery model called TriSys ASP built using Microsoft technologies. With this software-plus-services approach, customers can download the TriSys ASP software to their computers and connect directly to the solution through a remote desktop protocol.

All of the customers' information, customized forms and templates, et cetera, are hosted in the Cloud using XML-based web services. TriSys hosts and manages the application layer which is 100% Microsoft. The servers and the facilities, providing complete backup and disaster recovery services are managed by Microsoft Gold Certified Partner, DediPower, based in Reading, England.

 ## Sunny spells - the benefits

TriSys ASP provides massive benefits for entrepreneurs entering the world of recruitment because they don't have to procure hardware, software, or IT services. TriSys has more than 500 customers—and in excess of 7,000 users—in 12 countries around the world.

Currently, more than half of its customers have opted for the on-demand, software-plus-services model, citing recession-resistant subscription pricing, nearly limitless scalability with minimal cost, support of eco-friendly business initiatives, and the ability to work remotely from anywhere in the world.

Case study: Zoopla

Zoopla offers a unique real estate/ property website, offering information and tools to help users make better-informed property buying decisions.

www.zoopla.co.uk

 Clear skies - life was fine before the Cloud

In 2007, following the success of bringing DVD rental to the web with LOVEFiLM.com, founders Alex Chesterman and Simon Kain realized that the UK property market had yet to fully enjoy the benefits of the internet, particularly in terms of its ability to deliver transparency and efficiency. They set out with the mission to transform the property market via web services.

 Clouds forming - drivers to migrate

In their previous start-up, Chesterman and Kain built the server platform in a traditional way, from the ground up starting small and growing organically, with a few major step-changes in architecture along the way. "We learned that even with a decent-sized systems team that maintaining your own hardware platform is a time-sink and to do so within a tight budget can result in big constraints on responsiveness & flexibility," Kain comments.

"The cycle of procuring and installing servers or upgrades can be a distraction, especially when you're busy trying to make the company grow," says Kain. "It's very difficult to anticipate hardware demand under those circumstances, and the cycle of negotiating discounts, ordering, waiting for delivery, installing/configuring software, scheduling data-centre time to install the physical hardware – it's a drain on a growing start-up with tightly-controlled costs. And that's just server growth – unanticipated hardware failures can have a terrible impact on productivity."

Cloud cover – the Cloud solution

Zoopla developed its unique real estate/ property website using Amazon to host the services. Zoopla's aim is to provide the most comprehensive source of residential property market information in the UK, to help buyers, sellers, owners and estate agents alike and give them an advantage in the property market.

Zoopla's entire stack is hosted on Amazon EC2. For storage, Zoopla uses Amazon S3 heavily. Currently, every database table across all databases is encrypted and uploaded to S3 multiple times per day. Plus, S3 stores all user- and vendor-submitted images and data files.

Zoopla is currently testing some systems-management databases and their search technology on SimpleDB. And will soon be serving static content on Amazon CloudFront.

 ## Sunny spells - the benefits

In the first 12 months since launch, Zoopla estimates it has saved at least £200,000 in the areas of data-centre costs, server cap-ex, server upgrade/maintenance costs, sys admin salaries, network equipment, etc. According to Kain, the cost-savings, though significant, are not the biggest impact on a growing business. Instead the biggest benefit is flexibility and responsiveness. In total, Zoopla has saved hundreds, possibly thousands of hours of sys admin time, and more in terms of lack of downtime and reducing scaling complexities.

Kain sums up, "At Zoopla we have had significantly reduced growing pains in our first year due to AWS. The AWS team seems to intuitively get what we need to build our platform, and they don't dictate to us how we should build our platform. They make smart design decisions, and are helpful and responsive in support."

Results, not theory

Chapter

11

Final Word

A conclusion is the place where you got tired of thinking.

Albert Bloch (American Artist, 1882 – 1961)

CLOUD Computing has gone past theory stage. It is happening. Customers are demanding it and some ISVs are offering it.

Despite the hype it is not just an opportunity for start-ups. Everyone needs to understand Cloud Computing and make it a part of their roadmap going forward.

Now is the time to take action.

Appendix 1 – Book Summary

The Empty Raincoat: Making Sense of the Future

by Charles Handy

Paperback

Publisher: Arrow Books (1995)

ASIN: B000KKKHX0

The book's theme is inspired by a statue in Minneapolis that provided the title - are we just `empty raincoats' - units of labor and intellect - a cog in a corporate machine? Or is there someone of substance to fill the raincoat with meaning and purpose that goes beyond work?

"We were not destined to be empty raincoats, nameless numbers on a payroll, role occupants, the raw material of economics or sociology, statistics in some Government report", he writes. "If that is to be its price, then economic progress is an empty promise." Handy believes that it is every individual's challenge to fill their empty raincoat.

To make meaning in their life.

It seems that success - both professional and economic - comes with a disproportionate cost attached, not necessarily for the wealthy few but certainly for the remainder of society. This is one of the greatest paradoxes of our time. Handy's book, *The Empty Raincoat*, addresses this issue along with other paradoxes that, he says, we must begin to face and manage.

Life, says Handy, is full of paradox. Not everything can be understood, predicted or explained in full. One of the greatest paradoxes is the concept of choice. The freedom to choose for ourselves means that we have the ability to choose unwisely or wrongly. It is our challenge to manage the unavoidable paradoxes in our life, rather than strive for an impossible capitalist utopia based on individual material possessions.

Using colorful examples and analogies, the book offers a framework for the future of work and life in general. For organizations and individuals one of the first steps to change is the realization that business and personal security is not about land and buildings, but about knowledge.

The future will be owned by the workers because it will be based on their intelligence and know how - a difficult thing to gauge in financial terms alone. It will be like a 'virtual corporation' with a collection of permanent and temporary project groups existing more in a computer than in a set of shared offices. Work structures will be more about developing networks than honoring hierarchies and accepting responsibility not just blindly fulfilling core duties.

Handy uses a number of analogies to explain how these new structures could work:

The Sigmoid Curve illustrates that everything waxes and wanes; life, corporations, products, careers. It is critical to recognize where you are on the first S-curve plan to plan for the second before the first goes into decline. In today's fluid market that is more relevant now than ever.

The Doughnut Principle is a thought-provoking examination of work life balance. With the finite amount of time you have represented by the outer circle, the amount of time you devote to work is the inner circle - how thick do you want your doughnut to be?

And the Chinese Contract is about the contracts we make with ourselves and others - are they equitable or are we being selfish?

Appendix 2 – Book Summary

Why Killer Products Don't Sell

by Ian Gotts & Dominic Rowsell

Hardcover: 194 pages

Publisher: Capstone (January 20, 2009)

Language: English

ISBN-10: 1906465266

ISBN-13: 978-1906465261

Website: *www.killer-products.com*

We place tremendous value on our 600,000 partners, who help us deliver innovative solutions and systems to customers. We are providing our partners with compelling evidence about why customers who invest in the Microsoft platform outperform customers who don't, and we want them to know how to successfully sell their offerings to customers. This book gives them valuable, actionable go-to-market insights delivered in a very entertaining and readable style.

Allison L. Watson, Corporate Vice President - Worldwide Partner Group, Microsoft

According to senior IT leaders, innovation is a key to achieving competitive advantage. But it is an elusive concept and requires significant effort beyond mere invention – the ability to sell game-changing ideas that take a different approach. What this book spells out, illustrated by examples that leaders from every size enterprise can utilize, is that sales execution and proper positioning and packaging are the REAL competitive advantages for innovative products or services. These insights into the minds of buyers and what they expect from their vendors are supported with compelling evidence and fascinating anecdotes. This is a must read for executives at IT product and service vendors.

Dale Kutnick, Senior Vice President, Gartner Executive Programs

You're a major corporation with a track record of strong sales for your current product or service. You've worked long and hard to produce a unique offering that you know the market needs. It should have flown out of the warehouse, but sales tanked and it has hit the morale and commissions of the sales team. Why?

Alternatively, you are a nimble start-up with experienced founders, who have built their reputation on sales in previous large corporations. Again, you've developed a ground-breaking innovation and made some early sales. To really ramp up revenues you have decided to sell through the channel, or you've hired a hotshot salesman. But nothing is happening. The only sales are being made by the founders. Why?

It has long been understood that different sales techniques are required depending on the type and maturity of the product, the industry, size of customer, and the market. Some people think 'sales is sales is sales', and that any good salesman can simply change or morph their technique to suit the particular circumstance. But over 15 years of research into business-to-business sales has shown that this thinking is fatally flawed. There are sales techniques, but these are fine-tuning. What really make the difference are very four clearly defined 'buying cultures'.

The maturity of the product in the customer's mind determines which of the four buying cultures is appropriate, and this is most stark in the purchase of technology or software. So, it is not surprising that there is a startling parallel between the buying cultures and the Technology Adoption Life Cycle principles that Geoffrey Moore made popular in his books *Crossing the Chasm* and *Inside the Tornado* which focus on buying technology.

So to transform your sales performance you first need to understand where your product is on the maturity curve. If your product is disruptive or innovative it probably requires a Value Created sales approach to mirror the customer's buying culture. But what does this mean in terms of your company's operational culture, because the entire organization needs to be aligned to that culture?

The book paints a vivid picture of the operational culture of a company that is world class in selling innovation. It looks at it from every perspective; executive leadership, R&D, sales management and compensation, the 'sales animal', delivery and support.

But the authors understand that most organizations firstly don't recognize that buying cultures exist and therefore have little or no alignment. So, set out in a very practical and implementable 5 step methodology, are the actions that any organization needs to take to assess their current position, analyze the market maturity and then transform them to a proven business model.

The end result is an organizational culture which is aligned with your customer's buying culture, and positioned for stellar sales growth. Got right the results can be staggering.

So the final word goes to Andy Berry, General Manager at Fuji Xerox Global Services who sums up the benefits as.

"We achieved pretty well all we set out to achieve: our average deal size trebled, our largest deals are not only far bigger but there are more of them, and our resource usage is much better aligned. On top of this the main benefit was speed. I've no doubt this is what delivered a quicker return to the business."

Enough said.

Notes pages

Printed in the United States
151072LV00001BB/2/P

9 780956 155610